IN THE NAME OF THE PEOPLE

Liaisons

In the Name of the People
Liaisons
Transocean Partisan Research

ISBN: 978-1-942173-07-6
Library of Congress Control Number: 2018944086
10 9 8 7 6 5 4 3 2 1

Liaisons
liaisons@riseup.net / www.liaisonshq.com

In the Name of the People features a number of paintings (1992–1993) by Ben Morea, publisher of *Black Mask* (1966–1968) and a member of the Up Against the Wall/Motherfuckers (1968–1969).

Common Notions
314 7th St.
Brooklyn, NY 11215
www.commonnotions.org
info@commonnotions.org

Cover design by Josh MacPhee/Antumbra Design
Layout design and typesetting by Morgan Buck/Antumbra Design
www.antumbradesign.org

Printed in the USA by the employee-owners of Thomson-Shore
www.thomsonshore.com

For Clark Fitzgerald

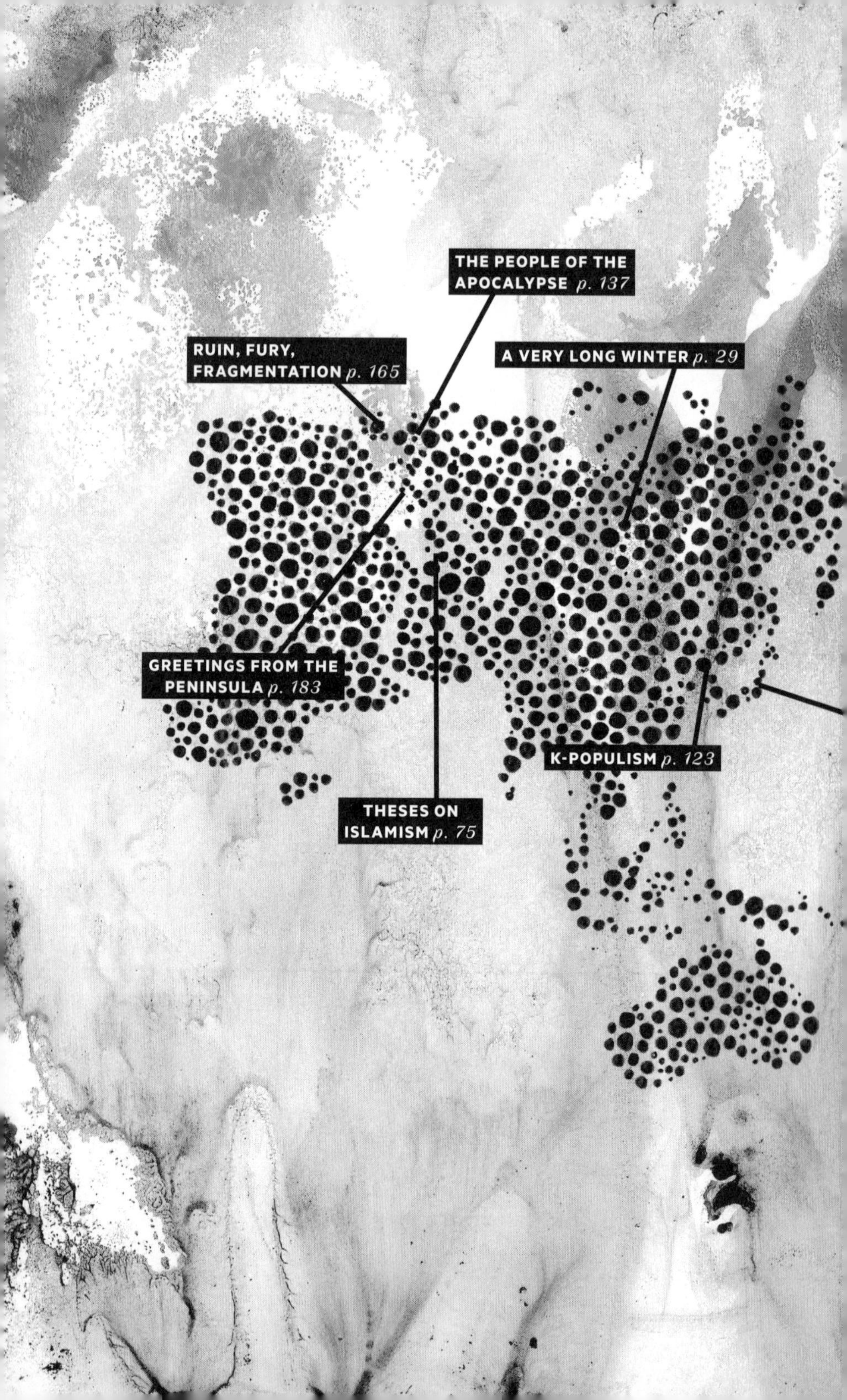

THE PEOPLE OF THE APOCALYPSE p. 137
RUIN, FURY, FRAGMENTATION p. 165
A VERY LONG WINTER p. 29
GREETINGS FROM THE PENINSULA p. 183
K-POPULISM p. 123
THESES ON ISLAMISM p. 75

INTRODUCTION

In *Liaisons*, an old dream reemerges from the depths. After years of elaborations, debates, connections, and political artifacts, our transoceanic endeavor takes form. We have found friends with whom we share a sensibility and a similar way of asking questions: How can we construct alliances without compromising what we hold close? How can we make room for different sensibilities without succumbing to moralism? How can we hold together urban struggles and rural autonomy? Certain subterranean affinities demanded a common place, a sounding board, a planetary reverberation.

The very hour the world returns to us as a dramatic unity through its own dissolution, the horizon of a humble international takes form. This is recognizable by way of a series of familiar developments: the multiplication of riots against the police, the generalized desertion of institutions, the blockade of nuclear and gas infrastructures, the proliferation of zones to defend, and the commoning of the means of life and resistance. Everywhere an awakening of political vitality and strategic perception, everywhere wanting to have it out once and for all—no longer with the world, but with its end.

We came of age in an age of separations, prisoners of an end-nearing time. Our political heritage is preceded by no testament, and this is all the more true of a world being devastated "to the last gram." In the sixteenth century, one spoke of *disaster* to designate the loss of a connection with the stars, as both points of reference and of influence. A few centuries later, D.H. Lawrence would make of this the cause of his and his contemporaries' solitude. They had, he wrote, "lost the cosmos. We lack neither humanity nor personality; what we lack is cosmic life, the life of the sun in us and the moon in us." The stars, by all appearances, have only dimmed since then. We find ourselves today thoroughly de-starred, *dés-astrés*.

In this context, the last of possible disasters is to believe they could all somehow be overcome. Such is the mirage of the populist, who comes to bring the situation under control, and just in time. Everyone was surprised by the victory of Trump, while Putin, Berlusconi, Erdoğan, Modi, and Netanyahu have reigned for years in the same register. Whether they hail from "popular" roots or have just acquired the style, this group exhumes that so-called alliance between the sovereign and his "People." They create the appearance of a gap on the other side of which the elites take refuge, huddled together under the obscure light of the "deep state." These new populists won hearts with the promise to safeguard all that, *in the People*, is identical to itself, in order to raise it, in unison, against the menace of the ethnic, sexual, or political minority—a gesture which often seems to extend to the point of including, at one moment or another, almost everyone. From the entrails of these masses long wandering in the neoliberal desert, they resurrect a new People of resentment.

We seem to have passed from a regime of war through pacification to one of war itself, almost without knowing it. Such a situation threatens to remove us from the agenda of things to come, of what *counts* or not, of what polarizes or evokes indifference. The enemy, no longer confined to capitalist dispossession, set foot at our door, threatening to pull the rug out from under our feet. The enemy sought to capture the very energies of opposition to the liberal order, to put them at the service of a governmental machine uninhibited of any sense of social acceptability. Far from bringing the refined techniques of governance of the "society of control" to an end, the new autocrats merely added a new helping of brutality. Justice openly conspired with the alt-right to shut down antifascists in the United States, the image of antifascist resistance was mobilized to maintain a "hyperreal" war in the Ukraine, and emergency laws were even established to suspend the French constitution. And all this happened "in the name of the People."

In the face of this convocation of the people at the altar of the Nation, the movements that rise up in response are also characterized as "popular," for want of more clear determinations. It is nevertheless clear, for example, that the *effervescence* of the Arab Spring or the French movement against the El Khomri law were largely due to the decay of unions and other classic organs of mobilization. Even at the podium of Nuit Debout in France, as with the Spanish indignados or Occupy in the United States, the meticulously articulated, formally democratic call to the People, crying out in the name of a totality, finally shattered through its own exhaustion.

We have seen, once the winds of the movement of the squares ran out of breath, new leftist populist machines rush onstage in a last attempt to save the good from the bad people. We have seen the capture and channeling of "popular" anger—for the benefit of a kingdom without foundation nor imagination—collapse in real time. And the enthusiasm evoked by Syriza,

Podemos, or Bernie Sanders for the prospect of a People supposed to suddenly awake from its anomie, take hold of itself again and reconstitute a heroic figure by bringing down the rising fascist beast—we have seen all this perish in a simple vote. Once again, the "People" have spoken.

All this makes one wonder whether the figure of the People still has anything to say to us, or if we should finally let it die in peace. For Marcello Tarì, the People will remain absent "as long as this present is in force. For now, the breach opened by revolt offers one of the few ways in which this lack can appear in the world, if only for the duration of a flash." It is really only these brief flashes, short durations of enthusiastic contagion—where the cruel absence of something like a People becomes the most glaring—that keep us from the postmodern cynicism so pleasurably proclaiming the end of every possibility.

If revolution is important to us, it is not in hopes of a new redistribution of riches or territorial control. Far from any discourse on political method, the age hardly leaves any choice but to think a revolutionary existence without subject, project, or heritage, including that "of the people." In a certain way, it consists of recognizing the failure of politics as we have always known it, even the politics we have loved. But an admission of failure is not an admission of impotentiality. Power designates that which has not yet come to light, and is up to us to bring into being. Liaisons desires to contribute to this task by opening a plane of transoceanic, partisan research. For Friedrich Schlegel, a dialogue is always "a chain or garland of fragments," and the intimate alterity of distant friendships is undoubtedly the best means of finding oneself again—by way of another.

In the middle of the 1940s, after having frightfully noted "the age of a finite world is now beginning," Paul Valéry prophesied a near future in which "nothing can be done without having the whole world interfere." Today, obviously, we're here. While the global interferes in the most minimal detail, the local takes on a truly global resonance.

It is also the case that ocean returns unto ocean, but in doing so is not the same. The infinite of the ocean always reveals itself in some sensible form: from the dramatic bursts of the Saint Lawrence through the violence of the Lachine Rapids, to the Seine's winding wander through wooded groves until it meets the English Channel, or the docile dispersion of the

Hudson into the Atlantic, under the glare of the metropolis' cruel gaze. Likewise, planetary political phenomena, whether planned or travelling by way of viral contagion, only imprint themselves on reality by embracing the singularity of local forms. In the face of each event that threatens its order, planetary standardization responds by way of a permanent restructuring, showing the extent of its latent tactical and strategic resources. Hence the urgency, in what concerns us, to consider these global phenomena in relation, but also to connect among and between them specific forms of local resistance and to construct situated revolutionary hypotheses able to resound millions of miles away. So as to not cede transoceanic communications to the enemy, we must take up a planetary conversation.

The question of knowing where a hypothetical revolutionary movement might stand today can only be considered by asking, if we are anywhere at all, *where we are*. This begins from the sentiment of belonging to the furthest thing, being linked and held by forces that exceed us in beauty and grace, opening us to our common worldliness.

— March 2018, between two continents joined by the Atlantic

SEPARATING SEPARA-TISMS

On Quebecois and Indigenous Nationalisms

> "*History*, in short, is what *separates us from ourselves*
> and what we have to go through and beyond
> in order to think what we are."
> —Gilles Deleuze, *Foucault*

To launch this new venture, *Liaisons*, we propose to share a series of local hypotheses from a transnational, revolutionary perspective. It has been said of the global era that it has allowed us to see "the entire world in a fragment." Every corner of the earth takes on an exemplary significance, which communicates a situated instantiation—and yet virtually universal—of the same world system. Even so, if the evolution of the system matters to us, it is less so for us to understand the system itself, but rather to understand what it seeks to attack. Ultimately, this enemy can only be explained by what it can't keep from destroying in order to grow. Partisan research thus must start by collecting from the rubble of the ruins of history, the living—friend and revolutionary alike—who never cease to resist their own unmaking. This foreclosure forces us to confront the most monstrous entanglements in order to find who, exactly, are our historical friends. Let us hope that by trying to unravel the ones that ensnare Quebec, others may be inspired to attack their own "national" demons, knowing that it is there where the critical details are hidden.

The situation in our corner of the world is indissociable from its history, invisible and yet so present. Crucially, "our" territory was the theater of the inaugural conflict of modernity, in the catastrophic meeting of foreign worlds. It was this shock, and the ensuing genocide, that illuminated the Enlightenment, which has never ceased to infiltrate the crooks and crannies of the globe. The clash between indigeneity and immigration has ravaged every part of the world, which further fuels the fire of current populist tensions. But the form it took here—that of the colonized colonizer—has produced a discontinuity between two secession movements: Quebecois and Indigenous. It is from this disconnect, from its separation between different separatisms on the same territory, that we wish to explore.

I: COUNTERFEIT

In 2012, we were struck by a student strike of an unprecedented scale. It overtook all of Quebec and provoked splits in every sector—even dividing families. In that instant, our reality was both transfigured and took on a more real consistency: the territory seemed, for a rare moment, inhabited. Everything was happening as if it was reaching a threshold: mass demonstrations, riots, a state of emergency, casserole movements, repression.[1] Then in the end, elections.

Capitalizing on the ambivalence of the casserole movement—whose insurgent character was confounded with the desire for reconciliation—the Parti Québécois, a nationalist-independentist political party that was "neither left nor right" won the bet *in extremis*. The rule of the Parti Québécois was a pathetic display, a series of operations seeking to deploy social rifts around an entirely different polarity, and thus convert the popular anger into a national unity. It attempted to institute a "Charter of Values" focused on "secularism," but clearly directed against cultural particularities (read: women wearing veils) and Canadian multiculturalism.

Despite the fact that this government did not last long—it was a brief pause of a year and a half in fifteen years of liberal rule—the effect of its ethnocultural repolarization with a republican-populist flavor continues to be felt to this day. The ascent of the intra- and extra-parliamentary xenophobic Far Right has not stopped, even as the memory of the strike has slowly been reduced to the charismatic figure of its principal student leader, who became a media star and soon after took the reins of a leftist, populist party inspired by Syriza and Podemos.

During the institutional reframing of the strike, we witnessed the systematic elimination of its eruptive and fragmentary character in order to transform the division into a new call for the unification of the People—be it the populism of the Far Right or of the left-wing media. The clearly grotesque nature of this outcome drove us to think through its historical basis. Along the way, Quebec was overwhelmed by the duration of the conflict, darkened by a profound instability that allowed us to see at what point the reaction

1. Inspired by the Chilean cacerolazos, hundreds of people took to the streets every day banging pots and pans in protest against police repression.

had deep "roots." Once menaced, the semblance of order revealed itself as the crystallization of a precarious historical compromise.

This hypothesis put us on the path of the past, in search of the tragedy of which the farce of 2012 would have been just the repetition. In the first place, it seemed crucial for us to take a retrospective look at such prior conflicts on the territory, to better understand the conditions of possibility as much as the emergence of their containment. To consider, in other words, how "the call to the people," a corollary of all mass mobilization, may allow a minoritarian people as well as a majoritarian People to occupy the terrain. Which underground communication made it possible for the plebeian energy of the 2012 strike to be so rapidly captured and reconverted into nationalist familialist resentment? This question is clearly not unique to Quebec and could equally address what happened in the aborted revolutions in Tunisia, Egypt, or Turkey.

Just as the populist mobilization had disguised the plebeian demobilization during the strike, the order that had preceded it had once been based on the camouflage and sealing of past conflicts, crystallized in social and institutional forms, but which were also equally cultural, psychological, and economic. Thus, to think through the longer-term story is also to think through the eternal return of its *counterfeiting*: both a triumphant falsification and plebeian counter-use. This is what we started doing with the Anarchives Collective, dedicated to exploring the forgotten archives of the revolutionary movement in Quebec. In excavating these ruins, which have received little attention, we have been surprised by the traces of an almost unknown legacy: a network of insurrectionary autonomy whose momentum had been thwarted by nothing short of a large-scale military intervention. This history had not been passed on to our generation except in the form of a cautionary tale, declared "terrorist" by the state to cover with the veil of tragedy the ways through which this past still speaks to us. We have discovered that there were many more affinities with our desires and forms of life than we could have suspected. In short: we were not alone, not on this territory, nor in this history.

Since 2013, through the Anarchives Collective, as well as a few public exhibitions and discussions, we have tried to continue that which the strike started—bringing a latent ungovernability into contact with its past forms—by reaching the spectral outlines of a plane of revolutionary consistency in Quebec. We have grasped this history, which they have taken to calling "separatism," as fragmentary remnants, which we must excavate through a work of anarcheology, to clear the many strata that make up our present situation.

If we approach the question of nationalism here, it is because it stands irreparably in front of us as soon as we address the relationship between history and territory. Often unbeknownst to their very creators, revolutionary situations are always accompanied by a counter-history punctuated by eruptive events—a counter-time—whose continued existence is incarnated in forms of adherence to territories—traditions—as so many ways to make use of and to inhabit it. Territory is not simply a place circumscribed by borders, even symbolic ones, but carries a plurality of ways to inhabit a given geo-biological assemblage. Emanating from the territory, these ways of inhabiting maintain a spectral presence, a retrievable one. Thus, any counter-history is, from the outset, counter-geography. But if the official history tends to spatialize time by folding in on a chronological timeline, the practice of counter-history—the anarchivistic—is an attempt at the temporalization of space, in order to restore it to the possible ways of inhabiting it. It acts, in sum, by extricating a counter-historical time, a time of *tradition*.

Opposite the study of these small territorialities stands—in a homogenous bloc—the occupation and then the development that we call "colonial," to which the narrative of the winners pays homage. Within this bloc, particularism and universalism—trying to threaten us with their infernal alternative—become the guarantors of each other, bound to each other's becoming where everything is done to prevent the fragmentary secession of imaginaries and practices singular to a place.

II: PLANE OF CONSISTENCY, 1970

In the collections of comrades' archives from times past, we have discovered a genuine plane of consistency, a network at the same time dense and diffuse, that from 1963 to 1970 was spread throughout the territory to the point that separatism was no longer a national question, but an existential one. For a brief yet dazzling moment, the program of the separation of the province of Quebec from the Canadian federation came to mean the separation of the "Quebecois People" from itself, revealing the *separatist* line of fracture within families, workplaces, etc. This break, which traversed the entire province, brought to light a multitude of existences and territories linked by a *de facto* independence: a collective autonomy inextricably material, ideological, and cultural, that diffusely grouped everything that differed from national unity to integrate a transversal alliance of movements of workers, students, and counterculture. The *nation* referred less to the entire population than to taking part in the separatist party. As writer Malcolm Reid states in his book *The Shouting Signpainters*: "A nation called Quebec was emerging from the snack bars of the east end of Montreal where it had been trapped under the name French-Canada. It was painting slogans on the walls, bombing federal buildings and monuments, flowing into the street . . ."

Since its formation in 1963, the Front de libération du Québec (FLQ) fought for national independence, mobilizing by any means necessary to that effect. In 1969, bombs exploded across the territory every two weeks—including at the Montreal stock exchange, in the mailboxes of rich anglophone neighborhoods, in a factory on lockout, or at an armory. The decentralized structure of the FLQ made it a particularly difficult target for the police to pin down. Its multiple cells, which seldom knew each other, each had their own broadcasting outlets—as many as ten distinct publications, addressing themselves to students, workers or the unemployed.

In 1970, after an extremely tense year in Montreal, where the power of the revolutionary movement had led the liberal government to ban assemblies (using laws of emergency in many ways similar to those used in 2012), the FLQ launched an operation aimed at expanding outside the metropolis to the distant regions of Quebec. In order to connect to embryonic struggles in different parts of the territory, FLQ cells opened a series of spaces across the province, strategically situated on the road taken by vacationers in the summertime. Some of these places, like the Maison du Pêcheur on the Gaspesian coastline or the Ferme du Petit Québec Libre in the Eastern Townships—initially established by the Free Jazz Ensemble of Quebec, whose musical experimentations colored political ones—attracted hordes of young people to issues of counterculture as well as activists in the area, and provoked aggressive confrontations with local bigwigs. The proliferation of these gathering points augmented the potential to form a movement by providing a series of zones of open condensation.

In the summer of 1970, having extended its decentralized network from Montreal to the whole province, and benefiting from considerable support from the general population despite its violent tactics, the network of the FLQ and its allies gave the authorities serious cause for concern. This was especially true since its conception of independence did not involve the idea of constituting a state—and hence, any possibility of political negotiation—but rather obtaining independence promptly and through action, instantiated through a network of communes, armed groups, and popular committees. Moreover, this network was tuned into struggles on an international level, through its alliances with the National Liberation Front in Algeria (where the FLQ had an "embassy"), the Popular Front for the Liberation of Palestine, the Black Panther Party and various groups of the American New Left, in a unique confluence where the most ardent nationalists turned out to be the most significant internationalists. It was at that moment that the concept of a "nation" became more of a call for genuine experimentation than an institutional demand.

In September 1970, following a hot summer throughout the province, the Liberation cell of the FLQ kidnapped the British diplomat James Richard Cross, demanding the liberation of their political prisoners in exchange for his release. The FLQ followed the example of their Palestinian comrades—with whom many of their members had trained—choosing kidnapping as a strategy for mounting tension. Faced with the authorities' refusal to negotiate, the FLQ's Chénier cell doubled the stakes by kidnapping the minister of labor, Pierre Laporte, known for his links with the mafia and his crackdowns against the labor movement. In response, on October 16, 1970, the Canadian government, directed by Pierre Elliott Trudeau (the father of current prime minister Justin Trudeau), decreed the War Measures Act, instituting a state of emergency suspending civil rights and sending the Canadian army into the streets of Quebec. Some five hundred arrests and warrantless searches of the extreme separatist Left were made. Within weeks, this vast shock operation succeeded in criminalizing all the militant organizations—even locking up union leaders—and scaring away their partisans, provoking a demoralization of the revolutionary movement.

The three letters FLQ soon became nothing more than a foil that History strove to reduce to a few political hotheads to cover up the vast array of those silenced by the state of emergency. October 1970 broke the alliance that was constructed among heterogeneous forms. The most striking example is the rupture that took place between the Far Left and the counterculture, the former of which later took the form of a rigid Marxism-Leninism, and the latter of which was characterized by a return to the land and a mystic new-age delirium.

III: AMPHIBOLOGY

Some forty years later, the hateful nationalist capture of the 2012 strike replayed this drama that formerly tore apart the independentist movement of Quebec. At the heart of the dispute was the Parti Québécois, a strange object that was both the culmination and the failure of a long maturation of the separatist movement in the 1960s. Between its foundation in 1968, when it was eager to exclude left-wing revolutionaries, and 1976, when it came to power, the Parti Québécois managed to capture the independentist forces and set itself up as a point of reference to replace revolutionary networks with its five-year plan of accession to constitutional independence. After handing over the independentist struggle to the state, which would "solve" the national question by developing infrastructures and Quebecois identity with language protection laws, the Parti Québécois progressively fell back on its old xenophobic foundations.

This nationalization of separatism ensured that all protests would therefore come up against post-Catholic familialism as the main form of Quebecois populism. Entirely extinguished by the institutional forces of the Parti Québécois, the nationalist movement gradually abdicated all willingness to address the question of autonomy except through the lens of incorporated economic independence or state independence acquired by means of a referendum—both attempts in 1980 and in 1995 were major failures. And as independence became a simple demographic-electoral question, everything that the separatist movement was able to put in place, in terms of capacities to immediately carry out independence, was relegated to the dustbin of history.

In the long story of Quebecois nationalism, this failure has been metabolized in the form of resentment against foreigners; within the referendum framework in which nationalism was compromised, the growing number of new arrivals to Quebec could not signify anything but the loss of a future independence referendum. The words of Quebec Premier Jacques Parizeau on the night of defeat in 1995, laying blame on "the money and the ethnic vote," created the xenophobic monster that has taken root in the historical depths of Quebecois nationalism, obviated in the decolonial detour of the 1960s only to return to the clerical-nationalism popular in the 1930s.

For that reason, if it is a question of measuring this failure—by the concerted effort of police repression and recuperation by referendum—it is advisable to make an additional inquiry into the archeology of struggle, in order to see how the division of what the FLQ was holding together was rooted in an older division, at the very origin of the modern movement for sovereignty. In the case of Quebec—except Montreal in certain regards—this modern movement dates back only as far as the beginning of the 1960s to what is called the Quiet Revolution, when the liberal party repatriated from within the state what was once under the purview of the clergy—first and foremost the education system. Before this secularization, Quebec paid the price of its defeat to its British occupiers, sinking into a long cultural lethargy, falling back on its Catholic faith, openly hostile to Protestant industrial development, but obviously submitting to British authorities. Feudal and ultramontane ideologies of *terroir*[2] that were promoted by the clergy then confined French-Canadians to powerlessly break their backs on their meager plots of land, banning any subversive literature, all to maintain an aggressively natalist politics to quickly populate a number of remote regions from land clearing committed by colonizers. From its infancy, in the post-war years, separatism had to position itself as breaking equally from the Canadian state and the institutions of the Great Darkness, which kept the Quebecois in a pusillanimous and stifling "colonized mentality."[3]

2. Particularly in the century between the 1840s and 1940s, *terroir* designated a specific set of values promoted in Lower Canada's literature, emphasizing a rural lifestyle centered on land, family, language, and religion.

3. The Great Darkness was a period of Quebec's political history marked by patronage and corruption, during the conservative reign of Quebec Premier Maurice Duplessis from 1936 to 1939 and from 1944 to 1959.

In this regard, it proved that separatism must first and foremost separate from its own society.

In the mid-sixties, the deadly yoke of the closed off French-Canadian finally gave way to the decolonial wave that shook the imperial world order. Eager for new platforms in a country untouched by counterculture, a group of young intellectuals and artists founded the magazine *Parti Pris* in 1963. The historical interest of this magazine is that it recognized not only its political and economic affinity with colonized peoples from Cuba to Vietnam, but also its psychological and spiritual affinity. This solidarity with colonized peoples led *Parti Pris* to understand their people as a "minoritarian society" who "never had a history: the history of others replaced it" (Paul Chamberland, *De domination à la liberté*).

Yet, if it was the impetus of the Quiet Revolution, *Parti Pris* failed to carry its own separatism to full realization, still haunted—like a good portion of other decolonialists of the epoch, Frantz Fanon included—by certain humanist-universalist reflexes, where a minority can only be realized and fully flourish by acceding to the majority. Thus, even if *Parti Pris* critiqued the impossibility of the colonized to understand themselves as separate from "the existence of its correlate, the majority"—that is to say the colonizer—whose project was described as "the building of a society founded on the suppression of a minority," this didn't stop *Parti Pris,* in turn, from enjoining the colonized to "the suppression of their minority status," toward the resolution of their contradictory being in order to reach the fullness of a majoritarian People.

As for the "socialist" character of the independentist project, it came to mean nothing more than a potentially infinite process of socialization, that is to say a perpetual extension of the state's reach, aimed at the cultural homogenization of a conquered territory. As a result, the critique made by *Parti Pris* against reactionary French-Canadian institutions gradually turned into a simple call for their modernization. Instead of becoming the so-called "Cuba of the North," we have found ourselves as merely the American Norway.

In the early seventies, the deployment of latent industrial capacities in Quebec *converted separatism into sovereigntism*, at once getting rid of all its fragmentary character. Thus the exploitation of resources, the establishment of distribution networks, and the construction of dams and highways materially embodied the national imaginary, providing the founding image of its national identity: the heroic tale of the brave Quebecois people taming the forces of nature to appropriate its powers and develop its infrastructures. Quebecois nationalism, after all, ended up acceding to the "majority"—by way of the great path of territorial appropriation and logistical-institutional majority.

But what was deployed in concrete and steel across the territory took hold *in place* of the separatist plane of consistency: energy independence, nationalized under the slogan "Masters in our own home!" After the October Crisis of 1970, in search of construction projects that could put the youth to work to take them away from the dangerous "negativity of unemployment," the Quebec government launched the most extensive hydroelectricity project in its history: the James Bay Project. As with each crisis in the history of Quebec, the counterinsurgency strategy compensated with further advances in the backcountry. As it was growing up, the Quebecois People gave itself the right to expropriate the Indigenous inhabitants of the territory, justifying their colonial advances as having "much to catch up on" compared to other modern nations. The victimized rhetoric of nationalism thus served to silence the existence of other peoples. In opposing the pillaging of their ancestral lands through judicial contestations or physical blockades, the Native people, in turn, came to put the brakes on the great deployment of the Quebecois nation.

IV: SEPARATING SEPARATION

In the summer of 1990, Quebec lived through another big traumatic uprising of a character that nationalists have neglected to take into account in the whole period of glory of their Quebecois nationalism. When a golf course in the village of Oka, a suburb of Montreal, planned an extension into the neighboring pine forest of Kanehsatake, in Kanien'kehá:ka territory, the Mohawks reacted strongly by blocking the main road linking their reserve to the French-Canadian village of Oka. In solidarity, the community of Kahnawà:ke, another Mohawk reserve in the area, blocked a bridge that led to the Island of Montreal and that passed through their territory. In the shootout that ensued, a police officer was found dead. The police retreated in panic, and their vehicles were set on fire and piled on the barricades.

Thus the Canadian Army took the place of the police, as is often the case in conflicts with Indigenous populations in America (Wounded Knee in 1973, Gustafsen Lake in 1995, etc). Faced with *Natives*, no half-measures: the foreign and impenetrable character of their resistance forces the colonial society to treat them as a foreign nation, which could not be overcome by a simple police operation. In this case, the Oka Crisis saw the Canadian Army encircle the Mohawk barricades with tanks, mortars, machine guns, and helicopters, until their adversary, at the end of their food supplies, was exhausted.

Now, in the surrounding Quebecois society, this crisis of almost three months would be the scene of a strong reaction of suburbanites, who responded to the blockade of the Mercier Bridge by staging racist riots, burning the effigies of Native people, and assaulting Mohawk families who took flight during the conflict with stones. These demonstrations of racial hatred, encouraged by certain "patriotic" media outlets, revealed to what point Quebecois society is keen on well-functioning infrastructure. Under the slogans "Masters of our own home!" (which had first served the nationalization of electricity) and "Quebec for the Quebecois," Quebecois nationalism in this way turned into anti-Indigenous reaction, assuming—as far as possible from separatism—the point of view of a majority society bent on suppressing all dispute.

If the course of the history of revolutionary independentism ruptured in October 1970, it was in 1990, during the Oka Crisis, that the parentheses definitively closed. Confronted with an internal separatism, the Quebecois people reacted with a violent tension, accompanied by outpourings of racist rage and cheers for the police and the army. The Quebecois minority, finding a constant in the history of anticolonial nationalisms, inept in its language and profoundly lulled by feelings of victimization, transformed all the more easily into a mass of hatred and resentment when faced with another difference that challenged its hard-won national unity.

On the anarchivistic level, the study of the Oka Crisis has brought us to explore the existence, within the province of Quebec, of territories that already have a *de facto* autonomous existence, separate from the majoritarian society. Vast and numerous territories, extending far beyond densely populated zones, drawing a completely different geography made up of reserves, hunting grounds, and contested zones, whose consistency—unlike national territory—is fiercely heterogeneous.

Not only are there a good dozen Indigenous "nations" that cut across "Quebecois" territory, but these nations break down into more than fifty communities, each having its own dialect and habits and customs. Moreover, these communities often find themselves separated into a number of different factions, at least in part because of the effect of colonial blackmail. The coexistence of traditional structures of governance and state-imposed band councils as its unique agent and interlocutor form the matrix of this Indigenous factionalism, further complicated by the historical stratification of multiple forms of cultural and religious reconciliation. In the Mohawk reserve of Kahnawà:ke, for instance, one counts no less than four longhouses (traditional community centers) for a population of less than ten thousand inhabitants, some following the Iroquois Kaianerekowa (The Great Law of Peace), others the code of Handsome Lake marked by Quaker influence—and this doesn't even include the Christian churches and the official Band Council. Decidedly, separatist multiplicity—a double-edged sword—is inseparable from Indigenous culture.

This, at least, tells us the history of the American continent, which one can reread as a single push to impose a homogenous conception of territory and government on Indigenous populations that are resolutely fragmented and, subsequently, ungovernable. Few historians today dare to affirm the validity of any of the treaties formerly passed between the heavily armed colonial forces and a handful of so-called "chiefs" who were handpicked and awarded the title on the spot.

There could be no central government on the territory of most of the northern pre-Colombian Indigenous peoples for the simple reason that the territory was conceived of as anything but a kingdom, on account of an impossibility that was as much logistical as symbolic (the two going together). From one end of the continent to another—on Turtle Island—one phrase continues to ring true: "the earth does not belong to us, we belong to the earth." Some add: "as we belong to our mother," the feminine principle having, in the territory of a matrilineal people, an intrinsic connection with the earth, such that the exclusive right to make decisions that concern terrestrial life are reserved for women, men playing the protective role of the sun.

First of all, among the Iroquois, matrilineality means that the man, once married, must move to the family of his spouse and all their children belong to this maternal home through the clan system—which constitutes just another level of separation. Based on the maternal house, the clan indicates family belonging through animal spirits: turtle, bear, and wolf being the three main clan families in several northern nations. These animal figures carry not only a symbolic line of descent, but a veritable *ethos*, implemented by the traditional systems of government as a specific responsibility vis-à-vis their communities. Accordingly, the bears have the tendency to be in charge of provisions, where the wolves have a penchant for politics. But the most interesting is without doubt the fashion in which the clans, beyond their filiation and exogamous function, intersect not only the communities themselves, but also linguistic families. Thus an Anishinaabe beaver is bound by a spiritual affinity with an Iroquois of the same sub-clan, bypassing their national, cultural, and genetic belonging: ethical affinity supplants ethnicity.

As we see it, far from a modern conception associating territoriality with community confinement, the essentially fragmentary character of the Indigenous conception of "a people" is associated with a large capacity for mobility. Just as the gendered polarization is not necessarily associated with sex, territorial belonging is not limited to lineage. Very much to the contrary, the way in which Indigenous peoples name themselves overcomes the genetic divide, moving it to the level of their traditional mode of living, which embraces the specific uses of a given territory, in all its shapes and forms. To the generic name of "veritable human beings" (*Onkwehonwe* in Mohawk, *Anishinaabe* in Algonquin, etc.) follows a definition linking them to the soil: the Mohawks are "those of the land of flint," as the Senecas are "those of the big hill," the Oneidas "those of the standing stone." Thus the people does not just designate the territorial fraction of a generic species, of which indeed only the white men—these souls without bodies—are excluded. At this point, and from this perspective, it can no longer be a question of "Nation," a concept that emerges from *birth*. The blood-right is invalidated by the earth (mother), to which human beings belong.

It is necessary to take the full measure of what differentiates this nomadic conception of territory, defined by usage without claims to property, from modern nationalism, on which Quebecois nationalism is dependent, as well as much of anticolonialism (through Marxism). In the absence of borders—and against those who traverse numerous communities in their hearts (provoking daily conflicts between the border guards and the traditionalists who refuse colonial passports), the nomadic mode of impropriety involves an intensive dose of circulation. It is only through perpetual movement beyond one's "plot of land" that nomadism can hope to attain an exhaustive understanding of the interdependence of natural processes in their smallest ramifications, an intelligence whose spiritual counterpart is animism, and whose political consequence is the rejection of development.

Nothing could be further from progressivism, obviously. Yet it is not any more conservative than progressive, since this nomadic conception by definition is in constant movement. For in the absence of movement, all that is solid melts into air: the trail of hunting tracks would be lost, the animals would not offer themselves anymore, the connections with other peoples would be poisoned, and isolation would lead to entropy. Songs and stories would soon be lost if a continual remembrance, a migration of thought in the mode of transmission, did not constantly call them back to memory. So goes the movement of tradition, which is forgotten as soon as it loses contact with the other to bring the self back to its original otherness. Such a practice, lost to some, will return to them through others, who will lose it in turn if the first ones do not come to remind them. This is because nomadism is the quintessential form-of-life of contact, which revives tradition at the point of touch: the time of tradition is carried in the flesh.

According to Deleuze and Guattari, if the nomad is the "one who does not depart" (*A Thousand Plateaus*), the tradition's necessity for contact is far from confining beings to their immediate environment: on Turtle Island, the fluxes were considerably distended, at the level of the river network that supplies most of the continent, from the Yukon to the Mississippi. But the fact is that despite the distance, these relations passed inevitably through touch. For example, the presence of Cherokee culture (from the southeastern United States) among the Potawatomi (based at the south of the Great Lakes) would not have occurred without the movement of real bodies having traveled—through an effort hardly imaginable to us—up to "their" territory. As a result, the relationships found themselves to be highly exposed, in all of their vulnerability, as well as—if we are to think in terms of power relations—their violence.

Our hypothesis is that the reason for this necessity of contact in a nomadic-animist regime, which makes Native separatism an ungovernable tradition in the eyes of the imperial powers, lies in its self-destituent nature. The art of proximities, as a situation-oriented ethics, is a mode of non-government characterized by the material impossibility of a concentration of prestige beyond a certain threshold that would enable it to reach subjugated subjects. This is the nature of what Pierre Clastres calls the "continual effort to prevent chiefs from being chiefs, it is the refusal of unification, the endeavor to exorcise the One, the State" (*Society Against the State*). Here, there are no more subjects than there are objects, but one purely subtractive multiplicity (Deleuze's "n – 1"), where decisions (under the traditional horizontal systems pillaged by American democracy) *take the time they need.*

This idea is crucial in order to grasp the intrinsic difference between destituent separatism and constituent sovereigntism. In a "materialist" perspective—in a sense much broader than Marxism understands it—the constitution of a mode of government capable of projecting and imposing its operations on distant peoples must be understood through the material means by which it spreads and enforces itself. If relations, within the mode of non-government proper to a time of tradition, are held in the flesh, the governmental regime of colonial time must *disincarnate* them. Which is to say, turn them into inert matter, disanimate them. Animism, however, does not know any "matter" as a separate category: matter is always already there, living and shaped in a way that is inseparable throughout all relations—familial, ritual, political, or hunting. The first colonists, who landed on Turtle Island imbued with a scholastic-intellectual tradition, had only such inanimate matter on their minds, most of their thought struggling to distinguish it from the soul. Thus, from the outset, they searched for that which they could develop on this continent, an attitude that only intensified over time, while 95 percent of Americas' Indigenous population was annihilated. Only then could the romantics mistake a cemetery for a "wilderness" (William M. Denevan, *The Pristine Myth: The Landscape of the Americas in 1492*).

Against the tradition of contact—against all tradition—particular to a territory, colonialism had to substitute an empty and abstract space to make place for the infrastructures that would take the place of traditions once held in the flesh. This relegation of contact to infrastructures would tend toward an inexorable monopoly, which continues to be pursued today through those infrastructures that we fallaciously call "virtual." By forcibly changing relations—which then become "social"—to make themselves the go-betweens, the infrastructures and facilities obstructed the possibility of contact in favor of this inextricable entanglement of optimization that we call technology. Evidently, the maintenance of this system of interdependencies presupposed and required the constitution of a state to ensure its functioning. In this way, contact turns out to be more separatist than infrastructure, insofar as it immediately and entirely carries in its smallest fragments the entirety of a culture.

This phenomenon is the logistical setback of the materialism applied by Benedict Anderson in his reading of the emergence of modern nationalism (*Imagined Communities*). If Anderson reveals the determining role of print capitalism—first and foremost the daily newspapers—in the constitution of the homogenous time and language through which a national entity can be imagined, his focus on the field of representation leads him to underestimate the infra-symbolic material conditions that allow it to unfold. Newspapers, which inculcate the feeling of a quotidian continuity in a given cultural unit, would be nothing without the roads—and eventually the trucks—that distribute them to the four corners of the "imagined" nation.

Benedict Anderson's analysis—which attributes the imagination of the nation primarily to the unification of language brought about by mass printing—allows us to pinpoint what, in separatism, "makes a difference." In effect, in indigeneity, it is not only because of the extrinsic links between the different dialects, whose contact only increases their heterogeneity by creating Creoles and Pidgins, but also the internal articulation of languages that creates the possibility of a "nation." The encounters between Europeans and Native Americans is so recent that Native languages have been able to keep their structure relatively safe from colonial syntaxes. In spite of modern attempts to annihilate their use of their own languages by educating Native children in colonial residential schools, the vestiges of these languages offer rare examples of an adherence between spoken word and territory, of which they are the symbolic and sonic expression. Some Mohawk traditionalists say that their language tunes to the telluric frequency of the territory from which it originates, echoing its plants, animals, and uses at the specific resonance of a given geographical constitution.

Could it be that the structure of Indigenous languages themselves contain something that resists the colonial matrix?[4] This would explain both the colonizers' relentless effort to exterminate these languages that are unfit for trade, as well as their astonishing survival five hundred years after contact. The practice and memory of these languages has become essential not just for cultural transmission and the history of a people, but also as a real support for the match between a mode of life and a vision of the world—a shared truth.

On the other hand, the fact that colonization and the operationalization of language is still ongoing even within our own Indo-European languages allows us to believe that they might carry something else, something like a mode of living that resists—a nomadic language inhabiting the perpetual movement of the verb. We would have to break open our language from within (using as much etymology as poetry) to see how Indo-European languages could only have become colonial through the force of a long history of struggles crystallized in language. This still leaves its traces in even the smallest of our statements.

V: JUNCTION

It is up to us to distinguish this originally animist "accursed share" presumed at the basis of any culture, and that which is a part of the colonizer mentality, in the sense of a perceptive structure able to project an abstract space-time and extract an isolated noun to which it can fix its infrastructures.

4. An inquiry would be needed on the role of tonal and verbal languages, largely present in the Indigenous world and in which intonation plays a determining role in meaning, which marks the recalcitrance of these worlds to colonization. The agglutinant or polysynthetic character of these languages suggests that a non-ownership conception of territory could be carried within their structure, which presents a surprising absence of subjects as much as objects. These are replaced by a potentially infinite agglutination of adjunctions, prefixes, and suffixes, which situate the expressed reality in relation to a series of symbolic orders: temporality, localization, gender (often much more numerous than the two sexes), position of locution, etc. Thus, these languages might well conjure the possibility of landing on a substantive noun having full ownership over itself: they would discern their object by its contours, a game of mirrors and cross-references where narration identifies the living reality.

In this case, everything seems to oppose Quebecois and Indigenous separatisms, except their common opposition to the British Crown. Historically, it was only for the sake of its collapse that they converged, if only periodically, centuries ago, at the cost of fratricidal wars with other Indigenous people. This is why the question of alliance is extremely delicate. More often than not, it amounts to the minority people only strengthening the ranks of the stronger element. The Two Row Wampum, created by the Iroquois in the seventeenth century, sought to delineate their relationship with white settlers. This beaded belt, setting a juridical precedent for the Iroquois, shows two parallel lines, which represent the respective rivers of two peoples, each standing in their own vessels: the Natives in their canoe and the settlers in their ship. Thus the alliance first and foremost requires the recognition of an unalterable heterogeneity: to be a shaman overnight—to play the sorcerer's apprentice, in short, apart from one's own cultural baggage—is no less colonialist than pressuring for development. We will have to find within our own boat that which will make it sink. For it could only be self-sabotage: the so-called "sovereigntist" tendency, irresistibly inclined to unify itself into a self-identical homogenous society, is the worst enemy of its poor parent—the separation of a minoritarian people.

This means that the fault line even passes through the notion of autonomy itself, which can have either a constituent or destituent form. These are two respective ways of grasping the absence of a People, either trying to reach it by synthesis or subtraction. Here lies the crux of the problem of the Quebecois People, being a minority in Canada but a majority in its own right. In one gesture of declaring independence, in this case, it may simultaneously evade the oppressor, and (all the better, they will say) oppress its own minorities. We must believe that the separatist problem is eminently a question of scale. And thus it points to the logistical consistency of governance—the scope of power being in proportion to its technical capacity to reach the territories it intends to subjugate.

To the extent that colonialism is opposed to all tradition, tradition can only appear to us in a fragmentary state, not just in the sense of ruins doomed to wither if they are not revived by contact, but also in the sense that it holds divisibility as an essential characteristic. If the current tendency of capital seems to lean toward fragmentation, this can only be explained by its will to track down all that escapes it in order to bind it to its never-ending technological growth. That is the defining aspect of liberal colonialism—British style, the only style, after all, that has really worked—to let the local powers go about their business as long as they continue to pay tribute to Empire. The fragment could not escape the reach of Empire, and thus remain a fragment, except by dividing itself at the slightest approach, showing still another side of the coin, twisting in on itself like a Möbius strip. The narrative of Quebec identity that considers the historical phenomenon of trappers—these fur traders who once deserted French colonies and disappeared into the woods to join in Native ways of life—as the proof of some privileged link between the French and Native populations often neglects to acknowledge that those who deserted would risk the death penalty if they returned to civilization. Only a faction can combine with another faction. Society, as a whole, is incorrigibly homogenous.

However, if we must admit a fragmentary character in the French colonization of the continent, it is contingent on the cowardly manner in which this colonization was conducted. As a mercantile settlement without any will to populate (contrary to New England), the first French-Canadians were extremely dispersed and vulnerable on the territory, which delayed the progression of homogenization for some time. This was true not only in their relationships with the Indigenous peoples, but among themselves. The first "inhabitants," as they were called, did not speak the same imperial French that is familiar to us now, but Breton, Poitevin, Norman, and Occitan—without even taking into account the Irish, German, Finnish, and other peoples that immigrated to the new continent before disappearing into a single English-speaking bloc.

This fragmentary legacy highlights three things that we will outline in conclusion. First, there exists the eminently fragmentary character of orality, prior to the unification of language through print. This not only applies to spoken language, but also to the nature of story, which in the oral tradition is subjected to the contamination of contact and the fate of mistranslation. In written history—the Hegelian journey of the Spirit, at the end of which lies the synthetic horizon of the State and its New Man—there is a whole forest of spoken histories, event-based and situational chronicles, each time repeated, born anew.

Secondly, there is the crucial fact that the fragmentary escapes the categories of colonial understanding, which can only comprehend it as savagery either to train or exterminate. Paradoxically, this implies an absence of operational distinctions specific to Western culture within the fragment. The fields and disciplines which are integral to Western culture, namely the political, cultural, and religious, seem impossible to dissociate in the fragmentary perspective—which is infinitely divisible by the effect of another fragment, and not of that which advances into a totalizing bloc. Hence the singular opacity yet thriving character of the fragment in the eyes of settlers. On this point, there is no doubt that the most powerful moments in recent political history, such as the separatist decolonization of the Front de libération du Québec with respect to Quebec, owed their vigor and strength of conviction to their surprising capacity to hold together revolutionary politics and counterculture in one experimental movement. In this period, when independence was achieved by the deed, it was understood that autonomy requires—at the very least—not to be disarticulated by external categories, and therefore not to respond to the language of the enemy.

Finally, if there is really a tradition that we will never cease to carry on this continent, it is perhaps precisely our lack of traditions specific to the territory. That is to say our properly *immigrant* character. Let us not forget that the latter is distinguished from the colonist precisely through its minoritarian and un-constituent character, by its own impropriety. But what would it mean to (re)take charge of our immigrant condition, the one that was once the lot of renegades fleeing the old continent infested with plague and famine? At the very least, this would imply inquiring once more about the uses and languages specific to this place, which would become foreign once again through our stay.

But above all, to assume our immigrant past could lead not to national appropriation but to a secret passage between indigeneity and exile. Because the continent, rediscovered by exiles, might very well approach the freshness that was always already felt by the first. Whereas the Indigenous people see themselves as sojourning in the territory, no less than exiles, beyond—or rather below—all property, at the root of indigeneity, there is perhaps no self-sufficiency but rather the constant need to renew the link, to keep contact. And thereby becoming-people, irreducibly minoritarian.

A VERY LONG WINTER

On a warm summer evening in Kiev, my friend told me a story about his grandfather. The story takes place during World War II in Ukraine. As a peasant, his grandfather found himself in German-occupied territory after yet another German offensive. His grandfather wanted to fight Nazis, but needed to figure out how. There were two options: he could stay in occupied territory and look for a partisan unit, or could try to join the Red Army. He decided to find the partisans, which is how he stumbled upon a strange unit fighting the Germans. The story doesn't mention how, but he figured that these were Makhnovists.[1] My friend told me how his grandfather would vividly recount how he decided to stay as far away from them as he could, because *those people* would be crushed by both the Nazis and the Reds. The chances of survival in such a battalion were virtually non-existent.

Very little is known about this battalion today, but it was likely led by Ossip Tsebry—a well-known Makhnovist who fled from the Bolsheviks in 1921. In 1942, Tsebry returned to Ukraine in an attempt to build an anarchist partisan movement to fight both Nazis and Bolsheviks. While little is known about it, this unit did exist and was eventually defeated by the Nazis. Tsebry was captured and ended up in a concentration camp, then was liberated in 1945 by the Western Allies, and subsequently managed to escape the Bolsheviks once again.

We remembered Tsebry at the dawn of the fall of 2014. Russia had already annexed Crimea and was advancing troops in Donbass. At that moment, no one would have been surprised to hear that Russian tanks were moving on Kharkov, Odessa, or even Kiev. I had just arrived from Saint Petersburg, where I had seen how Russian society would actually fully support the invasion. There was no antiwar movement in sight, and as we exchanged words of remembrance among friends, our emotions matched the intensity of the situation.

TROUBLED WATERS

In the time that followed, the discussions revolved almost entirely around fascism and antifascism. All the other debates were overshadowed by

1. Followers of Nestor Makhno, the commander of the Revolutionary Insurrectionary Army of Ukraine, also known as the Anarchist Black Army, who led a guerilla campaign in southern Ukraine against other factions seeking to exercise authority over the territory (Ukrainian nationalists, and German and Russian forces).

the question: who is fascist and who is antifascist? Since the beginning of the Ukrainian uprising, Russian state propaganda stealthily resurrected the old Soviet vocabulary, declaring that those who were part of the movement were either fascists or Nazis, or were at least manipulated by them. Anarchists and leftists from the Ukraine responded by noting the Russian state is actually the region's most fascist state. "Fascist" volunteer battalions and the "fascist" Donetsk People's Republic (DNR) were all over the news. Antifascists from Belarus and Ukraine, Spain and Italy, Brazil and God knows where else all went to fight. Some ended up on one side and some on the other.

At first, Western leftists, seduced by images of Soviet Berkut[2] buses ablaze on the icy streets of Kiev, largely supported Maidan. But when they realized that the diagonal black and red flags were actually those of the fascists, they had a sudden change of heart and started supporting the "antifascist popular uprising" in the East. And then they saw *VICE's* feature about pro-Russian antifascists, who actually turned out to be fascists. This was all a bit too complicated for them, so they turned away from the Ukrainian situation all together. Yet the West was not the only site of confusion. Anarchists and leftists from Russia were arguing to death over who exactly was fascist and antifascist in Ukraine, as if this could explain everything and summarily resolve the matter at hand.

No one had any clear idea of what to do in fact, even on the ground. We were all desperately looking for guidance, especially in stories from the past. But the reality of war, and the general mobilization it entails, was not an object of analysis for us. Most of us grew up with the feeling that war wouldn't happen here. We felt like these things could only happen on the periphery—a space that we usually ignored or to which we gave little attention.

The only war story we were familiar with was the story of the Great Fatherland War.[3] That story, like all myths, was clear and self-explanatory. There wasn't much to debate, which made the war a powerful tool for manufacturing unity. That is how my friend and I came to remember the story of Ossip, today a story so neglected and forgotten.

2. Berkut is the most brutal unit of the Ukrainian riot police.

3. Also referred to as the Great Patriotic War, the Great Fatherland War is a literal translation of the name given to the part of World War II that was fought in the Soviet Union.

THE GRANDFATHERS' WAR

Our generation, which came into the world near the end of the Soviet Union, still remembers the myth of the Great Fatherland War. When we were children, we played at war—and it was always the same war. It was a war between us and the bad guys, the German fascists. We knew our enemy from the old Soviet movies. The new streets of my neighborhood, built in the eighties, were named after Soviet war heroes, and in the street you could never escape all the monuments of the great Red Army and the martyrs of the war. Some of our cities were even considered "heroic cities." My grandfather was a veteran, and for big events, he would proudly take out his medals to wear.

During the nineties, when the news was filled with strange camouflaged men with guns, I couldn't connect these images with the story of my grandfather and the monuments to the heroes. That war—the war of all the movies and the songs—was the sacred war. That war was full of heroism and purity. What we saw on television just seemed like a nameless bloodbath, a war full of confusion.

In "the country that defeated fascism," oddly enough, no serious theory of fascism ever emerged. For the common Soviet citizen, fascism just meant the epitome of evil and abjection. But in the subculture of prison gangs, for example, tattoos of swastikas and other Nazi insignia were considered symbols of a radical denial of the state. These symbols did not have the same meaning in the West, and in Russia, antifascism came to mean something different.

This difference was a question of onomastics, established first through the act of giving a name. In the Soviet Union, World War II was called the Great Fatherland War, and was considered, in Soviet historiography, as part of the eternal fight to defend the fatherland. The term "Fatherland War" is a name that was already used during Napoleon's invasion of Russia. In the late thirties, and even more so during the war, Stalin and his propagandists began to speak of Soviet history within the wider historical context of the Russian Empire. This propaganda constructed the narrative of an unending struggle against the invaders from the West: from Alexander Nevsky in the thirteenth century to the Napoleonic invasion in 1812. This glorification of feudal and aristocratic heroes would have been impossible to imagine even a few years before, but, for the purposes of mobilization, of course it wouldn't hurt to sacrifice a few principles. Because who, if not we, the *Great Russian People*, could smash fascism and liberate Europe? As the war dragged on, it became not only a fight against fascism, but a war against that insistent invader, who arrived again and again to conquer our sacred Russian land.

According to this logic, the enormous human losses during the war were not due to the failures of the Soviet state, but were a martyrdom of necessity. They were a sacrifice that fits comfortably within the old story of the God-chosen Russian Nation, humbly taking on the burden of others and saving Europe from eschatological disasters, again and again.

In the context of the repression of the thirties, ethnic deportations were massive. As this trend continued during the war, the deportations were justified through accusations of Nazi collaboration. Russian ideologists love to mention collaborator units formed by Nazis during the war, composed of different Soviet ethnic groups. By creating the figure of Traitor-Nations, they are able to omit the fact that most collaborators were actually ethnic Russians, in order to legitimate colonial politics and ethnic repression.

Through this revisionism, the state has successfully created an equivalency between the Soviet subject and the antifascist. By essence, a Russian is antifascist, and thus being against Russians means being fascist. Anybody standing against Moscow for any reason now became fascist by default. In this framework, victory could only be achieved through national unity, and being Russian meant being loyal. Now any protest against central power could be easily reframed in these simplistic terms.

RUSSIAN ANTIFA AND STATE ANTIFASCISM

While it has lost some momentum, in the 2000s, the Antifa movement was a significant mobilizing force for Russian youth. While it was a very heterogeneous movement, what its members held in common was the beautiful but not always well-calibrated desire to smash Nazis. The more this movement focused on the practical aspects of attacking the Right, the less it could propose any kind of significant theoretical framework to analyze fascism. What is worse is that its members often just ended up naming "fascist" anything they didn't like. This was the case for the gangs of youth coming from the Caucasus. These gangs not only challenged their hegemony in the streets, but also showed "a lack of will to integrate" and accept the power of Russian culture in the "historically" Russian cities. "Black racism" or "Caucasian fascism" became widespread terms within the Antifa milieu. A significant part of the milieu even had no problem calling themselves "patriots" and Nazis "spoiled Russians" who forgot their roots. As one of the most popular songs of the milieu proudly proclaimed: "I am the real Russian / You are just a Nazi whore."[4]

Consequently, these milieus could not produce any alternative vision of history that could pose a challenge to that of the state. They just repeated mindless mantras about the strange character of fascists and Nazis in the "country that defeated fascism," and bragged about having a grandfather who went to war.

Elaborating other narratives and representations, they believed, could undermine their reach and separate them from the "common people." They tried as much as possible to look and act *ordinary*. They wanted to distance themselves from any form of marginality. Some even assumed an avant-garde role among the "healthy" part of Russian society. Given the commonplace of this populist strategy, it isn't surprising that some of them began to sympathize with imperialist ideas, or even went to fight for the "Russian World" in Donbass.

THE RUSSIAN SPRING VS. MAIDAN

The 2014 Winter Uprising in Ukraine was deep and long. When former president Viktor Yanukovych ran away, the vast majority of those who took part in the movement were ready to stay in the streets to expand the Revolution of Dignity (the official Ukrainian name of the events).

Vladimir Putin's regime was in a delicate position. It had been dealing with a weak economy since 2012, and was still weakened by the protest cycle of 2011–2012. A protest movement so close to Russia's borders, and a successful one at that, wasn't a welcome event, but the regime had managed to create an internal unity and delegitimize every uprising and resistance. The Maidan events were not yet over when Russia annexed Crimea, creating a *de facto* war where there was a "popular" uprising and sending a message

4. This song, "What We Feel," was composed by the band Till the End, and features the band Moscow Death Brigade.

to neighbors that uprisings could weaken their country and make it easy prey for annexation.

The annexation of Crimea was met with a spectacular wave of nationalist euphoria. Since the independence of Ukraine in 1991, Crimea had been first on the list of territories to reclaim for Russian nationalists. After 2014, *Krymnash*, meaning "Crimea is ours," became both a meme and foundation for a new imperial consensus.

Two other important terms also appeared at that moment, although they are now all but forgotten: "Russian Spring" and "Russian World." Russian Spring was a direct reference to the Arab Spring, which Russian ideologists had declared, with the utmost seriousness, was nothing more than a special CIA operation against legitimate leadership in the Arab world. But the *Russian Spring* should have been the authentic uprising of the *Russian People*, willing to reunite under their leader and state as a part of the Russian World. As this potentially refers to any place and land historically related to Russia or with a significant Russian-speaking population, the scope of the so-called Russian World has always been unclear.

As with every populist idea, the Russian World was presented as something natural and self-evident—it was completely natural for Russian speakers to want to be annexed by the Fatherland. Through this discursive operation, it was not a question of the Russian Empire (re)conquering territories, but of the Russian people liberating themselves from the alienating rule of the West and coming back to the homeland. Apparently it was just like World War II, when the Red Army did not conquer new territories in Europe and Asia, but liberated these people from the yoke of fascism.

Through this lens, the annexation of Crimea simply became a "reunion," a manifestation of the unanimous will of the Crimean people to return to their homeland. Those who were not part of that consensus—like the native Crimean Tatars, for instance, who were well organized and protested the annexation—were simply ignored or seen as traitors. After the annexation, all the leftists, activists, and anarchists had to escape. Those who remained ended up in jail, or either just disappeared after a raid. Every public political activity became impossible. It's Russia, after all, and Russia means war.

THE PEOPLE'S ANTIFASCIST UPRISING

Different tactics were used to give the occupation of Crimea and Donbass the appearance of popular movements. In Crimea, where Russia has large military bases, it was easy to fill the peninsula with soldiers in a few days. These forces rapidly took over the most important infrastructural points, such as the parliament and the airport, after which they adopted an "observer" role to appear as a "peacekeeping" force to ensure that the "people's uprising" went smoothly, and that Russian-speaking populations were not "attacked."

In a disconcerting game of mirrors, pro-Russian forces started to copy the tactics used at Maidan. In the first days of the annexation, the "self-defense forces" of Crimea were created, copying the self-defense forces of Maidan. Officially, they were created by locals who wanted to defend their cities from the Nazi hordes allegedly arriving from Kiev. Of course, it was quickly shown that these self-defense militias were controlled by Russian officers. They were composed of Cossacks, local petty criminals, pro-Russian right-wingers, and red-brown activists from Russia. In reality, the self-defense groups and the Russian military operated together. During the assaults, plainclothes self-defense officers were performing all the actions, to portray for the media an image of the people's revolt. The soldiers were never far away, ready to step in if the Ukrainian security services or army intervened. This tactic contributed to creating the simulacrum of a peaceful and voluntary annexation.

The foundations of this communications strategy were laid during Maidan, while the Anti-Maidan movement grew in the eastern cities of Ukraine. At the core of this movement were pro-Russian groups, already familiar with Russian-imperial ideas. Anti-Maidan named itself an antifascist movement and repeated Russian propaganda's main clichés. Anti-Maidan's discourse was the inverse of Maidan: there were calls to join Russia, reinstall Yanukovych to power, celebrate the Berkut, and invite Russian troops to occupy the country. At the same time, there were also several ordinary people participating in Anti-Maidan—people who genuinely believed that a motley coalition of Nazis, homosexuals, and the American "deep state" had joined forces and seized power in Kiev.

At the beginning, Anti-Maidan presented itself as another movement against Maidan. One street demonstration against another street demonstration, occupations of state buildings against other occupations, one constitutive violence against another. On the ground, however, the realities of the two movements could not be further apart. In Donetsk and Luhansk, the Anti-Maidan movement acted with the support of local bureaucrats, the police, and organized crime. While Maidan was repressed, Anti-Maidan had free reign, and it helped the pro-Russians gain a significant number of official buildings and arms. "People's Assemblies," controlled by armed activists, elected "popular representatives." "People's Republics" were proclaimed, calling on Russian troops and holding referendums about joining the Russian Federation. Like in Crimea, all the key positions in these so-called republics were swiftly occupied by special officers and loyal activists sent by Moscow. The so-called uprising was over at that point, and a new life began in these "liberated" territories.

It is worth noting that when the clashes first started, when people were facing each other at the barricades, they often realized they had more in common than they thought. In Kharkiv, for instance, Anti-Maidan and Maidan camps stood in front of each other on Freedom Square. Maidan invited its opponents to come speak at the microphone to let them explain what they stood for, and in many instances people changed their minds and switched sides. This naturally upset radical nationalists from either side, who sought an image of a people's uprising, complete with its sacrificial victims. All that was a far cry from the mundane meetings, interminable conversations, and socializing that went on at the square.

To demonstrate which movement was a real "people's movement," both sides competed for hegemony in the street. This made clashes and provocations inevitable and increasingly violent. After the events of May 2, 2014, in Odessa, where more than 40 people died in a fire during clashes between Anti-Maidan and Maidan, and the start of the war in the East, protests in the streets stopped and many Anti-Maidan organizers went to Russia or the new "People's Republics."

Nevertheless, the project of establishing Novorossiya, an old colonial Russian name for some regions of Ukraine that were supposed to be reunited with the fatherland, was soon abandoned. The attempts to reproduce the "people's uprising" coordinated in Luhansk and Donetsk failed elsewhere, despite major Russian financial and media support. What remained, however, and continued to circulate, was the narrative of the popular uprising. With the help of the already familiar paradigm of the Russian Spring, the Donbass uprising was declared to be "antifascist." It didn't seem to bother anyone in Russia that the leaders of this "people's uprising" were composed of officers fresh from Moscow. After all, they were pursuing the mission of the Red Army: save the people from fascism and machinations from the West.

Antifascism is the key idea that bridges the old monarchist empire, the Bolshevik superpower, and the new Russian State: a world power that keeps getting stronger despite the intrigues of its enemies.

In this context, it's no wonder the war in Ukraine didn't incite large protests in Russia. On the contrary, the streets were filled with tents of solidarity associations collecting goods and money for the people's militias of Donbass. May 9, known as the Day of Victory, became the main state celebration in Russia. It consisted of parades, fireworks, people's marches, children who wore Red Army costumes and chanted slogans like "To Berlin, To Kiev, to Washington!" and "Thank you grandpa for the victory!" The conflict in Ukraine was seamlessly converted into an element of the narrative of the new imperial consensus.

AFTER 2014

Like most contemporary insurrections, Maidan took political milieus by surprise on both sides of the border. The Russian, Belarusian, and Ukrainian activist networks have always been in close contact, and though Ukraine was considered to have more liberty and less repression, the social situation was no less difficult than elsewhere. Yanukovych was trying to consolidate power and resources while at the same time imposing neoliberal reforms. When comrades from different countries met, we sadly joked that Ukraine would soon be like Russia, Russia soon like Belarus, and Belarus soon like North Korea. It seemed like things could do nothing but get worse. If somebody had proposed on New Year's Eve of 2014 that Maidan would become one of the biggest uprisings of the last decades in Eastern Europe, they would have been met with waves of laughter.

In the beginning, leftists and anarchists did not really believe in the perspectives opened by the movement. Some recalled the Orange Revolution of 2004 as a fool's trap that would only change the faces one sees on television. Others wanted to avoid getting paralyzed by over-analysis, and thought it important to take part in any popular initiative. And effectively, this is what Maidan was. In its experience, aesthetics, and composition, it consisted of a "popular" uprising.

Most of us, undecided, decided to wait. Our uneasiness came from strange slogans about "Euro-association," as well as the presence of the Far Right and neo-Nazis. And while the Right was not setting the agenda of the movement, it was better organized and was boldly trying to exclude its enemies from the square. All leftist symbols were seen as a positive reference to the Soviet Union, thus pro-Russian and pro-Yanukovych. As for the anarchists and other radicals, they weren't organized enough to participate as a distinct group.

By the end of December, the movement had grown but did not present new developments. It seemed condemned to be an endless encampment of cold weather and boredom. But in mid-January, the regime decided to scale up repression—emergency laws were adopted and the occupation was brutally attacked, causing several casualties. After the attack, the situation changed dramatically, becoming a struggle against a real dictatorship. Leaving their doubts behind, the radical milieus joined the movement.

They were rapidly joined by comrades from neighboring countries. We saw with our own eyes how Maidan's "Russophobia" was an invention of the Russian media. It didn't really exist. It didn't bother anyone to speak Russian at the barricades, even with the strongest Moscow accent. Some people joked that you might be a spy, but then usually added: "We will meet at the barricades in Moscow chasing off Putin!"

Maidan grew by waves, adopting more radical methods as more and more people got involved. From field kitchens to underground hospitals, fight trainings to lectures and film screenings, and transportation to distribution and supplies, a huge infrastructure was growing up around the protests. There were even attempts to compose decision-making structures, in the form of soviets or assemblies, but they didn't have time to take root. The Berkut started to openly shoot people in Kiev, and in February the insurrection spread throughout the country. People were occupying administrative buildings and everywhere blockading the police. The regime attempted a last push, but overestimated its forces and failed, and then Yanukovych was forced to flee to Russia.

In appearance, Maidan had won. An enormous amount of people in Ukraine gained experience in autonomous organizing and street sensibility, and sacrifice did not befall them in vain. People felt like the game had changed, and they could now take hold of a common power.

But, in anarchist and leftist circles, this euphoria soon died. Thanks to the efforts of the liberal and Russian media, however opposed they were in their ends, the Right was able to portray the image that it was the radical vanguard of Maidan. Among many of us, joy gave way to panic as those whom one might have fought on the street the day earlier had now suddenly gained official posts in the new structures of state power.

Something far more dreadful was on the way. Russia annexed Crimea and started a war, which was an ambiguous gift for the new government. The energy set free on Maidan was channeled into volunteer battalions and support for the ruined Ukrainian army, which couldn't do much against Russia. From now on, defending the Revolution of Dignity didn't mean being on the barricades of Kiev, but on the front line. The movement then disappeared, of course, as it is obviously wrong to protest when your country is at war.

As for the Russian leftists, they found themselves on the side of Russian propaganda, and began to increasingly criticize "Ukrainian fascism." Well-known figures like Boris Kagarlitsky started spreading stories about an "antifascist proletarian popular uprising in Donbass." Some of these leftist personalities could be seen drinking tea with Russian nationalists and imperial fascists at the next meeting for the Russian World in Crimea. The young went to war as volunteers, if not to bomb villages, then at least to take some selfies in camouflage, Kalashnikov in hand. Others became war journalists, following battalions like the Prizrak brigade in Donbass, whose leader, after rounding up a few well-known neo-Nazis, became famous for defending the idea of raping women who weren't home after curfew. None of this seemed to bother the Left, as long as the battalions kept waving red flags and singing songs from that sacred war, complemented by stories about NATO soldiers on the Ukrainian side and images of dead children. As for the older Western leftists, they found themselves reliving the Cold War and started support campaigns for the "antifascists of Donbass."

After the shock of the first months, most of the Russian radical milieus turned away from such a confusing situation. Either the issue of the war did not concern them, or they felt there was nothing they could do. There was also a new wave of repression in Russia, within a context of unprecedented support for Putin. In this situation, there was increasingly less public political activity, and more comrades turned to infrastructural projects like cooperatives or publishing. Others decided to immigrate, either within Russia or abroad.

In Ukraine, on the other hand, organizing was on the rise. Despite the war, political life was blooming, but things were shifting fast. The Antifa and punk milieus generally became patriotic right-wingers. Anarchists weren't spared from this dynamic, many of whom grew sympathetic to the "autonomous nationalists" of Autonomous Resistance, an ex-Nazi group from the barricades of Maidan that was now spreading a mix of anti-imperialism and concepts taken from the new Right. Following their logic, nationality was the same as class, and ethnic conflicts and even cleansing could be understood as a form of class war. They saw the war with Russia as an anti-imperialist struggle, supported the army, and applauded their members who went to war as heroes. Others followed a similar path. Though they started by unmasking the fascist character of the Russian state, they ended up arguing that the only valid strategy against the Russian invasion was to support the Ukrainian Army. By evoking the history of World War II, they mirrored the logic of Russian propaganda, accusing anyone who criticizes the Ukrainian government of being pro-Russian or, of course, "fascist."

Another part of the movement decided that, again in reference to World War II, when faced with absolute evil, it was better to collaborate with the devil. In today's terms, Russia was the obvious evil, and therefore collaboration came in the form of joining the Ukrainian Army or the volunteer battalions—in the end, supporting the government institutions. There were some of our now ex-comrades who went to war, or at least supported such a decision. It is certain that no one wanted to become cannon fodder for capitalists and the state. But, for some of them, it seemed like the only option left to fight the Russian invasion and the Russian machine. The most naive sincerely believed in the *revolutionary nature of the people*, and for a moment really thought they could agitate among the soldiers, convincing them to turn their guns against the government. The most cynical spoke about the opportunity to "gain war experience," while others just felt pressure and the need to do something. With their support of armed struggle against the military invasion, part of the movement drifted toward a fascination for anything military. They seemed hypnotized by a new world of Kalashnikovs and camouflage, in contrast with which everything else just seemed to fade from view.

The topic of war soon became dangerous to address. The propaganda was working not only in Russia but also in Ukraine. While those who argued against the war could quickly be labeled as Putin's agents, it also became illegal to make public statements against military mobilization.

A lot of people simply became tired of all the conflicts and left the movement. The country's economic crisis forced people to work more, snatching away their time. While the energy of Maidan continued to nourish autonomous projects, stagnation struck the heart of the movement at the same time Ukrainian society was in crisis and the government still hadn't completely regained control of the situation.

OTHER HISTORIES

In retrospect, it seems the movement failed to find a way to oppose the rising populist imperialist consensus, both in Russia and in Ukraine. And for this not only our weakness, but also the way we have defined priorities in these last years, is to blame.

Too busy fighting fascists and Nazis in the street, we did not develop a solid analysis of what fascism is, nor did we propose an alternative to the official history of World War II, which seems to haunt us at every turn. At the level of rituals and symbols, we finally followed the version advanced by the Russian state—the myth of the unity of the Soviet People against fascism. The narratives about other forces that confronted both Stalinism and Nazism—like those of the partisan movement that rejected the rule of the Red Army—have become marginal. We have likewise paid too little attention to the conflicts of peasants and workers against Stalinism, or to the Gulag insurrections during the war.

On the other hand, we also must rethink the colonial character of the Russian and Soviet empires. Armed conflicts in distant places have so easily been forgotten. Even the war in Chechnya, which was important for anarchists in the 1990s and at the beginning of the 2000s, was forgotten by the next generation. We are in dire need of internal structures that allow us to transmit such experiences and their lessons.

In this light, it's not surprising that the explosion of war in Ukraine took us by surprise. We have not fully taken account of the fact that Russia is always at war somewhere, in some part of the world. And now this war knocks at our own door, and threatens our comrades and neighbors. It attacks our friends. We no longer know what common ground can establish connections between our movements, especially at the moment we need it most.

It seemed to us, as Russians and Ukrainians, that we almost lived in the same space, with a close past and present. We shared our experiences and resources in our struggle against common hardships. Yet when our states plunged us into war, feeding off the myths of our common past, we didn't know how to resist. The more they try to mobilize the dead to divide us, the more we should show that history can't be reduced to what is written by the victors. We ourselves have histories to tell—a story beyond imperialist myths, however they're assumed—because only revolutionary history will keep us warm during this long winter.

A PUEBLO,
A WORLD

On March 11, 1911, Otilio Montaño, a combatant of the Liberation Army of the South, took the main square of the Mexican town of Villa de Ayala with the cry "¡Arriba pueblos, abajo haciendas!" (*"Up with the pueblos, down with haciendas!"*). This proclamation, the heart of the Zapatista war of liberation, still resounds in each one of the *pueblos* that organize themselves to defend their territory.

What at first seems an irrelevant detail is useful for understanding the declaration's potential: *Zapatismo* didn't rise up against *hacienda* owners, or *hacendados*, but against the structure they managed. Then, as now, those who confronted each other weren't simply two classes or two groups of the Mexican population, nor even two ethnically homogeneous groups. The war of the *pueblos* against the haciendas was the clash of two radically distinct *forms of occupying space*; two forms of relating to the earth, to its fruits, and to its history. Two worlds.

Since the middle of the seventeenth century, the *pueblos* of Morelos, the state to the south of Mexico City that was also the site of Zapata's first stronghold, had been forced to retreat almost to the point of disappearance due to the expansion of sugar haciendas. The same space where collective life had been organized around *milpas*[1] and waters was now converted into a succession of agricultural farms, where the Nahua *pueblo* lived and died enchained by debt to their bosses.

Varying with local nuances, this confrontation consisted of a clash that was repeated throughout the country's geography. The history of the Mexican territory is none other than the history of how *pueblos* have organized to defend their collective life against those who want to convert their lands into a desert: against the haciendas and farms of the nineteenth century, but also against the open-air mines, wind farms, and tourism of today.

This is why it is no coincidence that Subcomandante Insurgente Moisés, the military leader of the Zapatista Army of National Liberation (EZLN), offers the apparently simple diagnosis: "the capitalist world is a walled plantation." This is also why comrades from the National Indigenous Congress repeat over and over that their struggle consists of defending life—that

1. The *milpa*, which involves a complex system based around maize, or corn, is the basic agricultural unit of Mesoamerica. It is a collective form that lies at the heart of agricultural life, with a very specific cycle and rituals and labors that revolve around it.

which is most simple, but also most intimate and potent. Because a *pueblo*—a community, an *ejido*[2], a piece of land—is always a form of collectively living a territory, a form of inhabiting it, caring for it and protecting it as if the body itself were its extension.

As in many other languages, the Spanish word *pueblo* ambiguously refers to a demographic unit, a group of residents, a multitude of dispossessed individuals or a solid political body. In Mexican Spanish, however, there is no such confusion. "Pueblo" was the word that attempted to translate the form in which the Nahuas named the places they inhabited: *altépetl*, a kind of simplification of a double metaphor: *in atl, in tépetl*. In the mountains, in the waters.

It doesn't matter if there is a town square or just a group of scattered lands covering a fragment of the sierra. A *pueblo* is the mountains, the valleys, the waters and the caves. Yet it is also, and most of all, the complex fabric of relationships taking place on this terrain: languages, work, assemblies, celebrations, conflicts, and deaths. There is no *pueblo* without territory, nor land without *inhabitants*.

Although they share a geographical position, a *pueblo* and a hacienda are never situated on the same territory. A mine or a highway occupy a point on a map in order to completely *depopulate it*. In contrast, a *milpa*, a spring, a path, or a river are places where the earth lets itself be inhabited, places where stories are created and circulated as well. This is why, for the *pueblos*, "the earth isn't for sale." Not only because it is the basic source of sustenance, but also because with its departure would go memory and all of life as well.

Topography, geography, and engineering are the only forms of territorial knowledge that the machinery of dispossession needs to operate. On the other hand, the wisdom of the pueblos *is incredibly more complex. In the rainforest of the Chimalapas, in Oaxaca, the Zoque have resisted invading ranchers for decades. They know to perfection the rainforest's landmarks and limits, and maintain all the legal records pertaining to Chimalapas topography that sustain their struggle.*

2. *Ejido* is the term the Mexican state used to legalize the agrarian reform in the 1917 constitution following the Mexican Revolution. The *ejido* is a "concession" of the state to a group of land applicants who didn't have ownership, but only the use of the land. The highest *ejidal* authority is the assembly of *ejidatarios*. Because of its collective nature, *ejidos* were used by many Indigenous communities to legalize their communal lands. Even though the *ejido* still exists, in 1992 a law was passed to legalize the conversion of *ejidatarios* into individual owners, hence legalizing the sale of collective lands.

Yet their knowledge goes much further. They still proudly tell how, in 1986, they captured an invading farmer within their territory. He was the brother of the governor of Chiapas. Immediately, the state's forces blocked all the routes leading out of the region. Meanwhile, the comuneros *(communal land holders) made their prisoner walk through the clearings of the rainforest only they knew. After walking all night, they turned him over to the municipal chief while the army still waited, watching him come out of the forest on to the highway.*

This extremely precise and intimate territorial knowledge is impossible to understand from the city, the colonial artifact par excellence. What from outside seems an extraordinary feat of organization is nothing more than the everyday forms of collective life. When one asks a comrade of what the Indigenous Governing Council, a body proposed by the National Indigenous Congress, consists, it is not rare to hear that "it is *just* the way we organize, only now throughout the whole country." Condensed in this little "just" are centuries of learning. After all, a *pueblo*—geographically, demographically, and ethnically—is not a static unit but a space where life unfolds, and with life the creativity of resistance.

Contrary to what the *indigenismo* of the state supposed, indigenous communities aren't "regions of refuge." The war of dispossession and extermination has, of course, displaced the *pueblos* toward rocky slopes and inhospitable zones, far from the fertile lands where they lived before. Yet the *pueblos* aren't simply a product of domination over an inert and passive group of people.

They are, on the contrary, "regions of defense." They are places where, in the face of war, a long-term resistance has been organized. Although anthropology (old or new, liberal or Marxist) finds it fascinating to imagine these communities as closed, conservative places, in the *pueblos*' forms of organization it is possible to witness the capacity to advance at the right moment, prepare a rebellion in silence, or transform their interior and ingeniously manipulate tools from outside.

In October of 2017, María de Jesús Patricio Martínez, known as Marichuy, the Nahua woman the Indigenous Governing Council elected as its spokeswoman, began her tour of the country. "We are going to walk as the pueblos *walk," she said, "like when we have a celebration." In effect, struggle and resistance and patron saint festivals have always been organized in the same way. Days before they begin, so there is no lack of food, the families each bring their contribution.*

The entire pueblo *is divided into rotating groups, so as to allow for participation in community work without neglecting one's own responsibilities. In a chosen place, somewhere well-known to everyone, intertwined branches supporting strung hammocks are raised, as well as temporary kitchens functioning day and night. Around the fire, people meet and share news. This is how the festivals of the community's saint are organized, but also how a highway blockade, land seizure, and self-defense during days of tense moments are organized as well. In struggle and fiesta, all the knowledges and abilities of a* pueblo *are clearly revealed.*

The *pueblos*, then, are territories where collective life and struggle take place. Or, more precisely, places where life and struggle coincide and end up being almost synonymous. Territories where existence, in the face of a war of extermination, is already a form of resistance against the invasion of farmers, *hacendados*, miners, and, of course, the state.

This is because the *pueblos*' forms of collective decision-making not only prevent the formation of small states in their interior, but also keep the official institutions far from their dynamics and territories. Organization and self-government help prolong the absence of the state, not alleviate it. This is why discussions about inclusion/exclusion and state "recognition"—for example, the impulse of certain anarchist positions to repeat over and over that the EZLN "sought state recognition in the San Andrés Accords"—are so fruitless.

In fact, perhaps one of the most brilliant and complex forms of the *pueblos*' strategy has been the way they have occupied and repurposed "official" institutions in order to prevent the entrance of the state. Before the entrance of the political party system became one of the most severe obstacles to the organization of the *pueblos*, the *autogobiernos* (forms of self-government) had taken the form of religious brotherhoods and civil councils in the colonial period, agrarian authorities and municipalities in modern Mexico, or leaders' councils throughout all of history. Reclaiming the right to autonomy is nothing other than obliging the state to recognize the way in which the *pueblos* have been able to deceive it.

Santa María Ostula is the only Nahua pueblo on the coast of Michoacán that has been able to completely maintain its lands and autonomy. In 2009, the town's Communal Guard was reconstituted to recuperate 900 hectares that had been invaded by ranchers since the sixties. In 2014, the same Guard united with other self-defense groups from other regions of Michoacán, mainly composed of small landowners and ranchers, in order to throw the Knights Templar Cartel out of their community. Since then, the assembly not only elects its agrarian authorities but also selects members of the community for civil positions usually elected by way of vote or direct appointment. In 2015, for example, Ostula and its allies promoted the person who has been the municipal president, a position of local state office, ever since. The commander of the Communal Guard of Ostula is the president's head of security, a "public functionary" whose principal task since then has been to confront the army, the Marines, and drug traffickers.

Not only is the existence of *pueblos* itself a form of resistance, but their collective organization is also one of the finest and most complex forms of combating the state apparatus. Official spaces are always infiltrated to be deactivated from inside. Neither a hacienda nor a state share space with a *pueblo*. The latter's existence and organization is always, and necessarily, destitutive. This is why it's not a contradiction that the Indigenous Governing Council had its spokeswoman register as an independent candidate for the Mexican presidential election in 2018. Only those who confide in democracy and its institutions can believe it's absurd to not want to win.

In October of 2016, the General Command of the EZLN presented a wild proposal during the assembly of the twentieth anniversary of the National Indigenous Congress. They proposed the Mexican *pueblos* convene an Indigenous Governing Council, a national collective organ that would elect an Indigenous woman as spokesperson to register as an independent candidate in the presidential elections of 2018. The assembly took place behind closed doors, and around the auditorium there was nothing more than conjecture, rumor, and misunderstanding.

Some days later, the doors opened and the General Command repeated the proposal in front of those of us who were there as listeners. From the beginning, it was clear that the electoral battle was practically irrelevant. At the heart of "the proposal," as it has been called since then, there was a phrase that was repeated over and over again: *take the offensive*. Confusion and surprise were assumed even as a kind of attraction. "The idea is so absurd it makes you laugh and cry... but when you think about it, doesn't it make you want to do it just to fuck with them?" This almost playful challenge became one of the slogans of the Indigenous Governing Council: "We're going to fuck up their festival of death." In exchange, there would be another celebration, another rebellion. "When July 2018 comes, the candidate won't even be the most important thing. You'll see we have the force to put this country back on its feet."

The proposal seemed to be a perfect diversionary maneuver (*maniobra diversiva*): distract the cities and the media with a grandiloquent advance to allow for the organization and silent offensive of all the country's *pueblos*. From the beginning, all the force was directed toward the process itself. It consisted of consulting the *pueblos* in order to reconstitute the assemblies that had lost strength and have a campaign so that the pueblos could meet. Here the central point is clearing the path of an organization thought to be permanent. "This is, perhaps, the last opportunity we have to save the country."

In effect, for at least the last decade, the worlds that are the *pueblos* have confronted a level of violence that perhaps no one had ever before lived in the history of this country. The entire territory became a wasteland of graves, assassinations, disappearances, and torture, but also extractivism, highway projects, mines, fracking, and extensive forestry. As never before, the state and drug trafficking have come together to break the earth.

The proposal meant a counteroffensive response in the face of this war. And, as in 1992, in the Lacandon Jungle, the uprising consulted for months with the *pueblos* that compose the National Indigenous Congress. It was there, in the assemblies' complex discussions, where the proposal found its place. Even the conflicts were a sign of force. A comrade, for example, started the process with suspicions. She didn't find the electoral scheme at all convincing, and so she went to explain this and consult in her own region. She came back unconvinced, but confident in the force that had been created. Asking questions, discussing, and meeting together had generated a potential she hadn't seen in years.

The *pueblos* heard the proposal and discussed it, transformed it, and made it theirs. Meanwhile, in the cities, the announcement arrived in a different form, typical of the urban world, where it was heard there would be a presidential candidate and not an organization of *pueblos*; that it would be a "symbolic" candidature and not a proposal for struggle. Even in its most progressive version, reception of the proposal was at times ridiculous and frankly racist. Marichuy appears as a "moral referent," a "figure" whose only function is to be there, in silence, showing the political class it shouldn't rob or lie. What is resistance and even survival in the *pueblos*, in the city is a lesson in good manners.

In this way, the proposal traveled in two divergent directions, two different worlds. The diversionary maneuver seemed to have fooled even those who support it from the cities. In the country's urban areas, efforts concentrated on gathering the signatures required by the electoral authority to validate the candidature. Few collectives have organized themselves for anything more. In this way, the proposal adopted the form of the city: organization coincides with collective life under the form of absence.

The city is not the superlative of the pueblo, *but its antonym. In the same way that a* pueblo *is a collective form of inhabiting a territory, a city is nothing more than the administration of its* depopulation. *This is why, since the nineteenth century, citizenship has been the theoretical weapon with which liberalism has attacked the pueblos. In 1822, after a decree ended the "Repúblicas de Indios"—the juridical regime that recognized the existence of the pueblos during the colonial period—the liberal state wanted only one thing: disintegrate every form of collective life and convert all of us in to Mexican citizens. Thirty-five years later, the government of Benito Juárez enacted a law that ordered the disappearance of communal lands, giving way to the "golden age" of haciendas, when the* pueblos *were transformed into masses of landless workers. One of the most enjoyable symptoms of the historic schizophrenia of Mexico was the 2018 national elections, when Andrés Manuel López Obrador, who campaigned under the banner of Juárez and defended the arrival of Canadian mining, was accused by his technocratic adversaries of being a "left populist." Apparently, in Mexico, populism is the superior phase of liberalism.*

In the *pueblos*, the impact of the proposal has been radically distinct. In December, Marichuy visited the *Ejido de Tila*, a *pueblo* north of Chiapas that has lived autonomously for two years. The presence of the "spokeswoman" convened communities from the whole region. The streets were bursting with people, and the *pueblos* organized in small groups to register and occupy their places. The communities in which political parties and chiefs had already put an end to assemblies and communal lands drew close to observe *how* a *pueblo* is autonomous and free. They listened in Ch'ol, their language, to councilors of the Indigenous Governing Council.

The organization acquires its full meaning in the *pueblos* most besieged by the violence of the extractivism administered by the political parties. Far from constituted power, *there* the proposal of the Indigenous Governing Council loses its symbolic aura that the city finds so fascinating in order to *touch the earth* and become real. The presidential election becomes irrelevant when it is instead an urgent matter of throwing out the local government, or recovering lands, or organizing a communal guard. There, the proposal isn't a *moral* issue. It is simply the possibility of living with dignity without giving up one's land, life, and memory.

On September 19, 2017, an earthquake hit Mexico City—the country's crown of power, dispossession, and racism. Two days later, the army and the Marines were ready to put an end to the excavation of buildings, although there were still living people and bodies trapped inside. People organized to prevent their entry and to require the most minimal thing—to protect the life that was still present and recover the bodies of their dead. Their organization allowed the search to continue to its end. For a few hours, the city lived like the rest of the country, collectively defending the dignity of life and death against the machinery of the state. A week later, things returned to normal. Organizing oneself in the city means knowing both that even among the ruins exists a possibility of life and being able to make this visible even in the midst of catastrophe.

On more than one occasion, the comrades of the National Indigenous Congress have said that "only the *pueblos* can save this world." Understanding this seemingly grandiloquent affirmation is the most important of tasks their organization has given us. It is only necessary to understand that where there is a mine, a highway, a political party, or a city, there can't be a *world*, which is to say, a territory and a certain way of inhabiting it.

In this sense, hearing that the Indigenous Governing Council wants to "govern the world" doesn't sound so far-fetched and instead becomes a proposal of an endless simplicity. Governing the world doesn't mean anything besides saving it, besides defending the life that takes place in the *pueblos* and ensuring that something of what is there multiplies and proliferates. It means making the cities, dispossession, and death turn back in order to know whether it is possible that, right there, a collective life can still happen. A *pueblo*, a world.

DECOMPOSE JAPAN

PREMISES

From November 28 to December 3, 2017, the second annual gathering of Living Assembly was held in Kamagasaki, Osaka. The previous year the location was a farm in northern Kyushu, but this time it took place at the heart of the metropolis, in the ghetto of a day laborer and homeless population. Hosted by local activists, twenty-five Japanese, four Korean, and two French friends met, lived together, and shared their words and presence. All participants were engaged in creating militant autonomy in different territorialities: homeless camps, urban neighborhoods, farm lands, and a university dormitory, where they came into confrontation with local authorities, state power, and capitalist development in varied forms.

The premise of Living Assembly is to be a platform for mutual support among like-minded individuals and groups by exchanging resources and inspiration—both in spite of and thanks to our differences. This premise provides us with a moment to nurture interconnectivity among our lives-as-struggles in different places and to synchronize the territories of autonomy beyond the Japanese archipelago. In this gathering, all participants presented what they were doing, their problems, aspirations, and coming projects, according to a series of shared problematics: how can we induce a reverberation among the struggles that maximizes our *power-to*, without being captured by the capitalist/state apparatuses; how can we create a planetary network of communes, without being confined by national territories; how can we engage in the phenomena of Politics (with a capital P)—such as war, xenophobia, and nuclear power—increasingly imposed by states as a means to oppress, control, and destroy our thinking and acting in order to create a mass impetus beyond reactive protests (we are planning to write a full report on the second Living Assembly in the form of a letter to all of you dear friends).[1]

There was a clear contrast with the first Living Assembly held in 2016, which was an attempt to reconnect activists who had been split apart after the Fukushima nuclear disaster in 2011. There were a few layers of fragmentation in the milieu of anarchist and anti-authoritarian movements, which

1. For those readers who are not on our mailing list and wish to receive reports, please write to us at livingassembly@riseup.net.

had disempowered the pre-existing oppositional forces, while also preparing a potency for their recomposition.

For about two years in the wake of the disaster, we saw possibilities for a collapse of the regime and sensed openings for revolution in the midst of catastrophe. In this phase, a big divergence of the entire nation was initiated between those who confronted the catastrophe and those who ignored it, in terms of attitudes toward everyday reproduction during an unprecedented crisis. The former party included the direct victims of the disaster as well as those people who acted on the catastrophe by participating in the anti-nuclear actions and the projects that dealt with radiation contamination. They created a new situation that shook the status quo, while being accused publicly by the government and privately by those still clinging to the status quo. The divergence often caused tragic splits in existing relations: families, friends, schools, workplaces, communities, and society at large. At the same time, we saw the divergence as a moment for decomposing the hierarchy and order of nationhood and creating a new sociality.

After Shinzō Abe's administration took power in late 2012, the period of reaction began. The government has managed the unending disaster in order to sustain the existing political and industrial order rather than full-heartedly confronting it to reach a solution, all the while announcing a successful recovery to the public in Japan and abroad. Meanwhile, the first split appeared among our political friends, as some activists abandoned their extra-parliamentary politics and autonomous projects, and instead concentrated on electoral campaigns for liberal candidates, claiming that "to deal with a disaster of this magnitude, it is necessary to work with the government." While the campaigns were intended to send progressive and antinuclear politicians to the parliament, they were also motivated by a call for "all-nation unity" in confrontation with Leviathan, as it were. (Unfortunately, the campaigning efforts have so far been less rewarding for the progressives than the conservatives; in the parliament, the reactionary parties have been gaining more control and passing bills to reinforce the government's information control and collaborative military actions with U.S. forces). At the same time, a second split was also happening in response to the disaster. This occurred among (1) those who chose to wait before engaging in immediate action against the disaster and continued their ongoing projects, (2) those determined to travel to disaster-stricken areas to support victims and to organize nuclear workers whose own radiation exposure was at stake, and (3) those who were engaged in projects dedicated to protecting people from radiation, including DIY radiation monitoring, information exchange, and voluntary evacuation from the radio-contaminated areas. In the activist milieu, the second group was called "those who go north" and the third "those who go west," two figures of diverging orientations from Tokyo.

Living Assembly 2016 was an experiment to collectively experience the potency of "those who go west," based upon our hypothesis that the mass impetus of freedom from the fetters of national unity that bound the people in contaminated environments would entail possibilities for decomposing the apparatuses of the capitalist nation-state. Those who went west were nurturing a new form of life outside consumerist society and a new geopolitics in opposition to the capitalist/state mode of development centered on Tokyo Metropolis. Thus, we lived together for a month on farmland where projects to create new communities of evacuees were unfolding, and we discussed whether this impetus could create a new platform for mutual support among all other territorial struggles for autonomy. On one hand, we came to share the prospect of developing a collective life by learning from the locals and evacuees in Kyushu, a project that still continues among some of us. On the other, however, a discouraging conflict arose: a group within "those who go west," called Zero Becquerelists,[2] who held to "the principle of preventative measure against radiation," accused certain individuals and groups of "still" living and being active in the eastern part of the island of Honshu, including Tokyo Metropolis, and refused to collaborate with them.

This third split made us reconsider the event of the Fukushima nuclear disaster from a more nuanced stance than that of the prioritization of the protective measure for "life." Zero Becquerelism originally found its name through an assembly of singular voices of people who had experienced and fought against both the invisible and unknowable effects of radiation as well as the governance that sought to nationalize it.[3] These were nuclear workers,

2. The becquerel is a unit of measurement of radioactivity.

3. For instance, the central government demanded that local governments (prefectures and municipalities) share and incinerate radioactive waste from the disaster; the "Eat and Support Fukushima Campaign" was instigated by the Ministry of Agriculture, Forestry and Fisheries in order to distribute food products

reproductive workers, farmers, fisher-folks, sanitation workers, homeless people, informal workers, young people, and others whose voices attest to the complexity of radioactive contamination and the physical and mental challenges it imposes. People inexorably respond to radiation differently, according to their material and immaterial affectivity, precisely because it involves a metaphysical aspect in terms of its invisibility, complexity, and endlessness. Yet when Zero Becquerelism begins to ignore these differences and unconditionally adopts the "absolute justness of avoiding radiation" as a political norm, the singularities of lives in struggle are flattened out. Radiation becomes a transcendental object, and the movement creates a new religion. We became highly critical of this position. *By no means would we want to be radioactive Stalinists!*

During Living Assembly 2017, with this critical consciousness, we discussed the necessity of approaching the problematic of radiation as the moment to radically reconstruct our way of understanding and being engaged in the world—beyond the dichotomies of material/spirit or man-made/nature. We assume that this could reveal a new horizon for our battleground in an age of irreversible mutations of the planetary environment. First, it is necessary to recognize the ultimate impossibility of determining the effects of radiation—especially the internal exposure to small doses—in terms of the scientific causation authenticated in legal and political institutions. In this way, we should affirm heterogeneous responses based upon varied individual sensibilities.[4] Secondly, we must respect and work with the lives-as-struggles of those who live in varied places on the planet, affected by a varied quality and quantity of contamination: Fukushima, Tokyo, Chernobyl, Hanford in Washington state, Navajo land in the southwestern United States, etc. Thirdly, we should analyze radiation in terms of "political ontology," which takes into consideration both onto-metaphysical and techno-political aspects of radiation: the complexity of its traveling patterns, the virtuality of its effects on vital activities, the government policies of nationalizing it, the capitalist enterprises that commodify it, and people's struggles to

from the disaster-stricken areas; and the Ministry of Environment considers using radioactive waste as construction material across the nation.

4. This affirmation is also related to the difficulties encountered by victims of Hiroshima and Nagasaki in getting compensation and their unending court battles; we expect more and more similar cases after Fukushima.

nullify or be free from it. Fourthly, notwithstanding these provisos, it is still important to cherish the prospect of "those who go west" as one of the crucial experimentations for creating a revolutionary horizon against the capitalist nation-state. Upon these premises, Living Assembly 2017 embraced heterogeneous struggles for autonomous territory, sustaining the problematic of the struggles in and against the ongoing nuclear disaster.

JAPAN: THE APPARATUSES OF CAPTURE

The Fukushima disaster is felt by many as apocalyptic. This is not so much in the sense of the "end of the world" or the "final judgment" as the beginning of a long and irreversible process toward a radioactive planet caused by the uncontrollable leaks of radionuclides from unrepairable reactors. This inexorably makes us face the destiny of the world we create by living in a capitalist nation-state. In effect, it has functioned as another sense of the apocalypse—that of the "revelation."[5] The catastrophic situation in the first two years had to have etched a deep imprint of that which was finally revealed in the minds of the populace. The substance of the economically flourishing society people had long embraced as their existential horizon was revealed—a society built on a regime whose governance had been entrapped or double-bound by the dual faces of nuclear power. These two faces were the experiences of nuclear genocide in Hiroshima and Nagasaki and the utopian narrative of a perfect energy, until the Fukushima disaster gave a fatal blow to the latter. It was, as it were, a consumerist heaven built upon two hellish powers.

We believe that what has been revealed will never disappear, even though it has been increasingly overshadowed by more immediate spectacles circulated in the homogenized outlets of the mainstream media (such as the orchestrated euphoria for the Tokyo Olympics of 2020 and the escalating threat of nuclear war in the Far East). This revelation hits the nail on the head of the postwar capitalist nation-state, including its constitution. Its substance is an entanglement of material and immaterial apparatuses: the insular

5. This sense of the apocalypse is pursued by D.H. Lawrence (*Apocalypse*, Penguin Books, 1995, p. 59), as well as Gilles Deleuze ("Nietzsche and Saint Paul, Lawrence and John of Patmos," included in *Critical and Clinical*, translated by Daniel W. Smith and Michael A. Greco, Minneapolis: The University of Minnesota Press, 1997, pp. 45–46).

territoriality; the dual functions of nuclear power; the introverted pacifism (Article Nine); the symbolic emperor system (Article One); the homogenized media; the society of high consumerism; and Tokyo Metropolis.[6] According to one perspective, the specific arrangement of the apparatuses belongs to a postwar temporality, but the apparatuses themselves must be seen as products of a longer geo-history; they have been developed since the "closed nation" (*sakoku*) policy during the Tokugawa period (1603–1868), through to the phases of modernization since the Meiji Restoration (1868), the imperialist expansion into the Asian continent, the total war in Asia Pacific, servitude to the United States as one of its most faithful client states, and post-nuclear disaster governance.

While these apparatuses have functioned to sustain the introverted space of the nation-state, they were born out of and constantly recomposed by global power relations as well as planetary movements (geography, climate and cataclysms).[7] One of the main points of our analyses is the paradoxical dynamic of being a nation-state in the world: the nation-state's content is always about its interiority, but its form is always shaped by its exteriority. The fountainhead of Japan's introversion was the geopolitics that constructed the apparatus of insular territory over the archipelago.

The Japanese historian Yoshihiko Amino (1928–2004) pointed out that "Japan" is a construct in the process of modernization. The common notion that the territory of the nation-state was always inhabited by a homogenous people called Japanese is but a projection of nationalist historiography. In Amino's work, which effectively deconstructs the *Japan-ness* of Japanese history, he shows how eastern and western parts of the country followed different patterns of social, political, economic, and cultural developments, wherein the western part was more connected to the southern part of the Korean Peninsula, while the eastern part interacted more with the northern territories of the Asian continent. It also demonstrates how

6. Here we must add the modern Japanese language as well, which should nevertheless be the subject of another reflection due to its complexity. See, for instance, Naoki Sakai, *Translation and Subjectivity: On Japan and Cultural Nationalism*, University of Minnesota Press, 1997.

7. The Japanese archipelago is located on the Ring of Fire, and the political, social and economic systems of the nation-state have always been recomposed on the occasion of earthquakes. This is especially the case with the Great Kanto Earthquake in 1923, which triggered political reform toward a fascist regime internally, and industrial and military expansion toward the Asian continent externally. The question today is what the Fukushima event might trigger.

a majority of people—commonly thought to be farmers confined in an insular territory—actually included a large portion of Oceanic People, who were not only fishing but also actively trading and pirating over the smooth space of water, through the pathways from the rivers to the seas, among the series of islands and isles, and between the islands and various parts of the continent.[8] Seeing a map of Japan with this insight, we can easily trace permanent sailing routes from the northern tip of the island of Hokkaido to the Kamchatka Peninsula, from northern Kyushu to the southern part of the Korean Peninsula via the islands of Jeju (now South Korea) and Tsushima (now Japan), and from the southern tip of Kyushu to the Okinawa Islands by a series of isles and islets. This is the space of "planetary intercourse" of which we are deprived, living in the world consisting of a disjunctive synthesis of nation-states.

The age of archipelagic exchanges began to be foreclosed in 1600, when the Tokugawa shogunate came to power in the fortified city of Edo (today's Tokyo) in the Kantō Plain, also the front for colonial expansion to the territories in the northeast. The shogunate divided and ruled 270 feudal domains on the islands of Honshu, Shikoku, and Kyushu for as long as 260 years. After a hundred years of warring states, this rule stabilized the country with an institutionalization of dual power: the spiritual authority of the emperor in Kyoto and the executive sovereignty of the shogunate in Edo. The policy of national enclosure strictly prohibited foreigners from entering and local inhabitants from leaving the territory, and severely limited trade activities: it was this enclosure that shaped the introverted nature of the nationhood that still persists today.[9] This was, as it were, the building of an antibody to protect an internal organism from invading viruses. This was also the advent of the primary apparatus of capture: insular territoriality as a receptacle to confine the mindset and mass corporeality that had previously been traversing the open space of the archipelago.

In the late eighteenth century, increasing threats of the colonial West across Asia gave rise to nationalist consciousness, rousing the myth of a native and unbroken line of the emperor. In 1853, the U.S. Navy steamed four

8. Amino Yoshihiko, *Rethinking Japanese History*, translated by Alan S. Christy, Ann Arbor: Center for Japanese Studies/The University of Michigan, 2012.

9. Tetsuro Watsuji, *Closed Nation—Japan's Tragedy (sakoku)*, 1 &2, Tokyo: Iwanami Bunko, 1982.

warships into the bay at Edo and threatened to attack if Japan did not begin trade with the West. The turmoil in the process of reopening the closed door weakened the rule of the shogunate, which had already been overpowered by the coalition of rebellious domains in the southwest—Satsuma, Choshu, Tosa, and Hizen—domains which all advocated emperor nationalism to decompose Tokugawa feudalism. The Meiji Restoration in 1868 terminated the reign of the shogunate and established an absolute monarchy of the emperor under the hegemony of the coalition. On one hand, the "passive revolution" (Gramsci) restored the imperial sovereignty from the past. On the other, it introduced European institutions of the modern state and the military/industrial complex. This was a drastic shift of the objects of "civilization worship" from Asia to Europe. The apparatus of insular territoriality that congealed during the Tokugawa period worked *paradoxically* to facilitate the formation of the modern nation-state as its geopolitical basis, from which the military/industrial expansion could now be initiated. It is not too pointless to call this moment the origin of "Japan."

Japan was thus the only nation in Asia that successfully averted colonization by the West, and instead the state sought to compete with and even overpower Western colonial forces by intervening in Asia with the same colonial ambition—but with the territorial handicaps of a low rate of energy self sufficiency as well as periodic earthquakes. And these handicaps are what intensified its military aggression. Thus, its geopolitical relations with the world have always been twisted: though it territorially belongs to East Asia, the state has been fated to behave like the West. Its mindset toward its own industrialization has consistently disdained Asia as bare natural resources and cheap labor power (or even slavery), despite the long premodern history of dependency on it.

Beginning with the Meiji Restoration, state policy has been continually driven by the will to "wealthy nation, strong soldiers" (*fukoku kyohei*)—the national modernization slogan—both overtly and tacitly, before and after World War II. (The present prime minister Shinzō Abe is evidently driven by this will, while also watching the fluctuating temper of U.S. president Donald Trump). Japan's delusional expansionism that inflicted numerous atrocities on the people in Asia Pacific regions[10] was terminated by unconditional surrender in 1945, soon after the nuclear attacks at Hiroshima and Nagasaki and the Soviet Union's declaration of war. The militarist regime of emperor-fascism was defeated by people's resistance everywhere it invaded, and ultimately decomposed by the U.S. occupying forces. The postwar constitution came into force in 1947. It was allegedly drafted by the Japanese government in 1946, which was actually done under the threatening pressure of the Supreme Commander for the Allied Powers General Douglas MacArthur. As such, this included MacArthur's intention to make it look like the will of the Japanese.[11] This document holds two famous sections: the peace constitution (Article Nine), and the symbolic emperor system (Article One), both of which were designed by the initiative of Supreme Commander for the Allied Powers in negotiation with the remnants of Imperial Japan—*never by the will of the People.*[12] In the first place, the Japanese state was deprived of its sovereignty by the institutionalized disarmament as part of U.S. global strategy, which came to be reworded as "peace." Emperor Hirohito (1901–1989) was exempted from trial and persecution for his undeniable war crimes and kept on the throne as a symbol. A number of first-class war criminals were also pardoned due to their influential status across society. Both the Japanese and American ruling classes believed that the recruitment of these war criminals was necessary in order to prevent the national body from decomposing and the insurrectionary crowd from rising up.

During and after the Cold War, Japan was always under the tacit *protection* and *control* of the U.S. military, which made one-nation pacifism possible in the midst of a global power conflict. For the U.S. government, the Japanese archipelago has served as one of the most crucial strategic bases in the world, and manipulating the nation toward its preferred direction has been a consistent state policy. It has allowed the Japanese state and capitalism

10. The magnitude of Japan's atrocities was no less, if not more, than that of Nazi Germany, which included the Nanking Massacre: https://en.wikipedia.org/wiki/Nanking_Massacre, biological and chemical warfare: https://en.wikipedia.org/wiki/Unit_731, the total annexation of Korea: https://en.wikipedia.org/wiki/Japan–Korea_Treaty_of_1910, etc.

11. Eto Jun, *The Constitution of 1946—its Bind* [1946 Kenpo—Sono Kosoku], Tokyo: Bungei Shunjyu, 2015. Original manuscripts were published in 1980 in the monthly magazine Shokun.

12. In this sense, Japan's postwar period must be seen as the lost moment for peoples' subjectivation (or rebellion).

to expand their power-over by now concentrating on the economy, which was initiated through the bloody earnings of special demands made during the Korean and Vietnam wars.

The introduction of nuclear energy into civilian life during the moment of economic growth was largely due to the intention of the ruling powers of both the United States and Japan. Notwithstanding the successful results of nuclear attacks against Japan, the United States meanwhile had to shift its nuclear policy in the early 1950s after generational resistance to nuclear weaponry across the world and the Soviet Union's success in developing its own nuclear weapon program. In 1953, the "Atoms for Peace" policy was advocated by then president Dwight Eisenhower as an attempt to tame worldwide dread and rage against the weapon and create a positive image of nuclear power by developing the civilian use of nuclear energy. It was especially vital to instigate this shift in Japan, where a massive surge of antinuclear militarism *and* anti-U.S. imperialism arose after the Lucky Dragon Five Incident, in which a Japanese tuna fishing boat was exposed to and contaminated by nuclear fallout from the United States' Castle Bravo thermonuclear device test on Bikini Atoll in March 1954.[13] In order to push this policy, the U.S./Japan nuclear lobby waged bombastic media campaigns (including employing Walt Disney) and shrewd information manipulation by taking advantage of the social atmosphere during the time of economic growth and the permeation of mass media (namely television). It is said that the nuclear lobby was spearheaded by CIA agents operating within Japan's Liberal Democratic Party as well as major media such as the Yomiuri Shimbun newspaper and the Nippon Television Network Corporation.[14] The key rhetoric these campaigns employed to influence public opinion was that "it is the Japanese, the only victim of the nuclear bomb, who are entitled to the peaceful use of nuclear power."[15]

13. For more general context, see: <https://en.wikipedia.org/wiki/Daigo_Fukuryū_Maru>

14. It can be asserted that a certain number of Japanese congressmen, bureaucrats, CEOs, and commentators in the media are agents of the CIA. The CIA has an annual budget prepared to have them operate, which has long been an ordinary practice. This information has been widely circulated since the publication of Tetsuo Arima's book: *Nuclear Power, Shoriki, the CIA* (Tokyo: Shincho-Shinsho, 2008).

15. Seigo Hiroto, "Thinking of Japan's De-nuclearization," published in Senshu University Institutional Repository: <http://ir.acc.senshuu.ac.jp/index.php?active_action=repository_view_main_item_detail&page_id=13&block_id=52&item_id=3837&item_no=1>.

In 1960s Japan, various forms of popular uprisings synchronized and created an impetus toward a global revolution (1968): the strikes in coal mines, the farmers' defense of their land against airport construction, actions against U.S. bases, the mass movement against the war in Vietnam, international solidarity projects against U.S. imperialism, students' occupations in high schools and universities, etc. In mutual reverberation, these uprisings nurtured the collective will to confront the power-over of both the interiority and exteriority of Japan—as the global apparatuses of capture.

Post-Fukushima popular protest has unfortunately not followed that path. During the first two years and continuing until today, a full spectrum of struggles has unfolded, albeit under the shadow of the media spectacles of mainstream politics. These struggles involved actions such as anti-nuke demonstrations; blockades against the distribution of radioactive debris and the restarting of power plants; innumerable lawsuits against the government and TEPCO (Tokyo Electric Power Company); demands for medical compensation; commoners' radiation monitoring and information exchange; voluntary evacuation; organizing nuclear workers; etc. They were lives-as-struggles waged from varied "modes of existence" and positions in a "class complexity." For us, they continue to be important impetuses to empower.

The spectacle of large popular protest in Tokyo began a few months after the disaster, involved heterogeneous forces and opened possibilities for creating an event. Many participants felt that their actions were part of the global uprisings that had begun with the Arab Spring in late 2010. Eventually, protest was institutionalized as a weekly Friday demo in front of the prime minister's residence. In the early stages, the mobilization was dramatically successful. As the organizers restricted the action to strict legalism in favor of representing a "normal citizens' demonstration" in the media, however, it turned out to be pathologically tamed. (The first split among the activists appeared along with this tendency). The organizing strategy involved not only mobilizing people through social media, but also producing favorable spectacles for the main media, whose persistent role is to produce and reproduce homogenous Japanese subjectivity. As the Abe administration came to power, the Fukushima problematic itself gradually grew less covered in the media, and the target of protest shifted from everything concerning nuclear power to the policies of the Abe administration. The objective has ended up being the protection of the postwar constitution (especially Article Nine) against Abe's reforms toward remilitarization, which are consistently within the parameters allowed by the United States. In other words, the original target of protest—the postwar regime as the fountainhead of the nuclear disaster—ended up being the object to be protected.

In these protests, liberalism and nationalism are tacitly merged in contradistinction to the right-wing fanaticism mobilized under the slogan "wealthy nation, strong soldiers." In other words, these are frictions between liberalism and fascism, or nationalism and jingoism. Certain ideologues that support this movement obsessively attack the radical movements of the sixties and their offshoots—especially their revolutionary perspective—as vanguardism and antipopulism. Furthermore, the demos are guarded by a group of mercenaries, who physically exclude and oppress those of us who seek to expand the realm of street actions to create an event that maximizes the power of the crowd. The goal of the organizers is to (re)produce "normal citizens" by way of a well-controlled spectacle, thereby preventing an event from creating an opening in social time and space.

We certainly are against the remilitarization of Japan and the suffocation of civil liberty that the Abe administration has been undoubtedly scheming. *No commoners want to see the return of a militarist regime!* However, amidst a world in turmoil, we think that one-nation pacifism is not only insufficient but also deceitful.[16] As recent exchanges between U.S. president Donald Trump and North Korean leader Kim Jong-un attest, peace in East Asia could be pursued only via coordinated engagements between peoples in the Korean Peninsula and the Japanese archipelago, who would confront not only their local governments but also the United States, in synchronicity with the anti-U.S. base struggles in Okinawa and Jeju. We consider the urban spectacle of pacifist protest as one embodiment of the apparatuses that safeguard the society of the capitalist nation-state from decomposition. For a revolutionary perspective, it is crucial to understand the postwar constitution as the

16. The limit of the post-Fukushima peace movement is clear when compared with those in the sixties, including JATEC (Japan Technical Committee to Aid Anti-War GIs), which clandestinely aided GI desertion for the purpose of decomposing the U.S. military stationed in Japan for the war in Vietnam. The difference is between a peace that is passively given by the power-over and the peace that is to be actively achieved by our power-to. The militancy that existed in the movement of the sixties and that is lacking in today's movement is due to this difference.

central apparatus of capture devised on a global horizon that entraps the minds and bodies of the populace within the territory of an insular nation-state under the protection and control of U.S. global strategy.

QUESTIONS ON THE BATTLEGROUND

This is not at all to say we are unsympathetic to the crowd who participates in the antinuclear demonstrations. In fact, all of us have been a part of it. It is always important to be a part of mass corporeality, the origin of all events. Neither do we reject electoral politics entirely, which might be useful—but only when an extra-parliamentary autonomous power exists that can evaluate its effects to make them serve its own benefit. What we emphatically oppose is the way demonstrations are represented in the media and spoken of in political discourse, not to mention the organizing orientation—all of which work toward the desubjectivation of the heterogeneous crowds by confining them within the norm of being "good citizens" who protect the capitalist-democratic-emperorist-nuclear state of Japan.

Thus, keeping a strategic distance from the protest movement, Living Assembly pays utmost attention to and collaborates with the anti-spectacular struggles that operate within and against the apparatuses of capture—namely, the territorial struggles for autonomy that entail an otherness toward and lines of flight from the postwar regime. These struggles include those of homeless and underclass communities (mostly day laborers), ethnic minorities (especially resident Koreans), informal workers, sex workers, students, anti-U.S. base projects of Okinawans, and those who go west. In passing, the participants of Living Assembly include not all but most of these groups. In the present essay, we will not get into the details of their struggles, which we will reserve for another essay. Here, instead, we will only point out their common attributes in light of the post-Fukushima conjuncture.

These struggles—which we call *lives-as-struggles*—are based in specific localities: homeless camps, urban neighborhoods, farmlands, and a university dormitory, where living is equal to struggling. Their participants are more or less outsiders to Japan's civil society, but cannot be bundled together as one oppressed class—presumably excepting heightened moments of insurrection—because their ontologies embody a complexity or heterogeneity asymmetric to being a normal citizen of Japan. *They are the flows of trans-Asiatic corporeality, or the offshoots of the Oceanic People in the archipelago.* These existential and territorial struggles are not waged solely for a particular protest or campaign. They develop according to a longer perspective that sometimes lasts for multiple generations. The struggles inexorably involve various forms of creating a commons in autonomous territories. Thanks to their experiences, techniques, knowledge and resources, they nurture the necessary capacities to host a collective form of life: varied projects for autonomy as well as oppositional politics.

The ambition of Living Assembly is to create a projective cartography of these struggles that shows the way they could connect with each other and with the struggles in the Korean Peninsula as well as other parts of the world. At the same time, we are enduringly affected by the nuclear disaster and continue to learn from its revelation. We are thus confronted by the primary question of how to turn the catastrophe into a revolutionary moment. That is to say, we must discover positive aspects in the multi-faceted breaches caused by the disaster. From this, two practical questions arise concerning the creation of commons in autonomous territories under the material and immaterial influences of radiation: one regarding ecology (for creating commons) and another autonomy (for our lives-as-struggles to develop), both of which determine the horizon of our battleground.

The Fukushima disaster has certainly run cracks in the core apparatuses that sustain the integrity of Japan as a nation-state. Thereafter, while the status quo has been desperately patching them up or even turning them into a fulcrum for tightening the security regime and expanding capitalist development, the commoners have been striving to confront them full-heartedly through various forms of experimentation. The spread of radiation trespasses the insular territory and deranges the geopolitical order of "uneven and combined development," wherein the countryside's labor-power and resources consistently serve Tokyo's metropolitan function.[17] This spread is beyond and above the control of governance based on the territorial interests of the nation-state and even of the United Nations as the negotiating platform

17. For instance, the Tohoku region that includes Fukushima Prefecture had long provided Tokyo Metropolis with the resources of primary industries: agricultural, fishery, and forestry products; in the time of high economic growth, a large part of the land there came to be expropriated by industrialization and real estate investment; many farmers who did not own land lost their subsistence and migrated to large cities to be day laborers in construction, dock work, and nuclear power plants.

among various interests. The Pacific Ocean—a planetary common—has been minutely yet steadily contaminated by radioactive leaks from Fukushima Daiichi, and there is no power/knowledge in the world that can deal with it.

In terms of the national economy, the primary industries have been damaged most substantially by radiation contamination. There is no proper word for describing the devastation of farmers and fisher-folks. What to do with their products and subsistence has been and will be one of the most difficult questions. Remediating the accident will require myriad (endangered) workers and endless costs. TEPCO's deficit will be limitless, which is to be paid by the people via electricity bills and taxes. All of this will exhaust human and natural resources for years to come. Many countries have stopped importing food products from Japan, and an excess of oil and LNG (liquefied natural gas) importations has caused a trade deficit for the first time in thirty-one years. In the long-term, this economic burden could end the aims of working life—to have a stable job, two children, and a suburban house with a car—that the citizens of the allegedly middle class-centered society have conceived for themselves in the postwar period.

Notwithstanding all of this, we have learned that the use of nuclear power will never cease. Our hope in the darkness was miserably betrayed. Those superpowers that have access to nuclear development don't have any intention of giving it up. Before the accident, 442 nuclear power reactors in thirty countries produced 14 percent of all the world's electricity. This number dropped to 11 percent in 2012. But by 2014, 435 reactors were operating in thirty-one countries, and a further sixty-eight were under construction. This means that the influence of Fukushima was no more than a momentary blip. Why? The only plausible answer we can come up with for now is that competing capital and warring states remain tethered to the proliferation of its supreme power of heat emission or destruction, and that its uses are increasingly tied to an unstable world security and market regime. A now planetary subsumption of life is at stake through what is routinely and endlessly imposed as a number of competing national security and economic interests. In ensemble, they exert devastating effects on all vital activities on the planet. We are living a reality wherein no matter how many voices scream no to war and environmental devastation, the capitalist/state mode of development does not have an ear to listen. This is simply because it does not have a head—not even two heads as in the age of the Cold War—but consists of many heads competing and warring amongst themselves, and that yet form a collective drive toward all-encompassing crises of vital activities on the planet. Each head—or the state—insists on protecting and promoting the interests of local industries (capital) and citizens (nation), while these territorialized *interests*—which are radically distinguished from the *desires* of the wretched of the earth—develop synergetic effects of which neither nation-states nor the United Nations as their negotiating platform can take hold. *The world as logos—the order of nation-states—has been breached.*

The irreversible effects of small-dose radiation are imposed on an unknowable number of people for countless years to come. First of all, ionizing radiation mutates vital activities on the level of genetic code (DNA), which is transmitted to following generations. This is essentially alien to the idea of ecology centered on the web of organic lives, operating on the mutations of somatic cells or the trans-metamorphoses of molecules. Secondly, its effects betray the principle of the commons, wherein the wastes (or the negative commons) must be recycled within the community that has produced them, instead of imposing them on its outside (peripheries). The full picture of these effects is yet to be discovered. So far, the effects are gradually and slowly severing the promised rapport between the land and the people in the contaminated zones as well as around the mosaic patterns of hotspots. Along with other environmental devastations, they would cancel the fundamental promise of sedentary community based on uncontaminated and stable resources as commons.

Tragic as they may be, these effects trigger a radical shift in our idea of life itself—from the one based on the individual interest endlessly (re)produced in capitalist economy to the one of ephemeral yet singular being that is part of communal relations and life-chains or even in "inter/intra-action of myriad kinds" on the earth (Donna Haraway), including both organic and inorganic activities.[18] The age of apocalyptic communism has come. It is neither utopian nor dystopian but inexorably imposed at the beginning of the long-lasting end of the world. Among commoners, the shift is embodied

18. From the atmosphere to human traffic, radionuclides travel following all movements on the earth—both natural and man-made—while affecting them on a nano-level. Radiation is, as it were, the negative of the omnipresence of planetary movement.

in the development of a "minor science" regarding the reproduction of the body under the increasing influence of radiation as well as the experimentation of new communities after evacuation. In other words, the people have begun to develop new ways of creating the body and having a rapport with the land—though the outcomes thereof are yet to be seen.

Therefore, it is in the breaches of national integrity and the shift in the idea of life (as body) that the practices of territorial struggles for autonomy would have to discover a common ground. In the age of irreversible mutations of the planetary environment, we assume this common ground is the new horizon for our battleground. But the new horizon has not yet revealed its full picture; what we have gotten so far are only glimpses of it through the breaches of apparatuses that compose nation-states and the world as their catastrophic synthesis.

In a global context beyond the Japanese archipelago, the world as *logos* had already been radically challenged by two impetuses, one negative and one positive: (1) increasing catastrophes of all kinds—earthquakes, hurricanes, melting polar ice caps, the rise of atmospheric carbon dioxide, wildfires, radioactive contamination, and all other cataclysms—inflicted by the capitalist/state mode of development; and (2) the global uprisings as reverberations among the singular struggles or the *becoming ungovernable* of planetary commoners—from workers, minorities, the Indigenous, immigrants, to all victims of injustices by the capital/state power-over. On one level, they are entrapped in the territory of the nation-state—as we all are—but on another level, they nurture an impetus that escapes its capture and opens transversal connections amongst themselves toward a possibility of a planetary revolution. Significantly, this prospect is based on the actual tendency in recent years according to which uprisings of varied places have begun to reverberate—as if recognizing each other—without the command of an international organization.

Therefore, the breaches of national integrity are also those of world history. Does this mean that the age of politics of the world is over? Not quite yet, because we are still entrapped and increasingly exhausted in world politics. Nevertheless it is clear the ontologies of our lives-as-struggles cannot be subsumed into the ontology of the world organized by capitalist/state development, because the essence of the revelation is the asymmetricity of the former to the latter. Perhaps we are in an endless transition from the politics of the world (as the political economy of nation-states) to that of the earth (as the spatio-temporal complexity of all events).

For now, we can at least say that our view of the interconnectivity of struggles is no longer grounded in the homology of internationalism based upon the politics of the world, wherein all national movements gather to form a unified institution toward a communist world, but the multitude of autonomous territories, small to large, in the countryside and the city, establishing transversal connections from neighborhood to neighborhood in an unending process of communization over the never conclusive movement of the earth. Our geopolitics is no longer based upon the present model for the formation of the world, wherein enclaves of national territories are absorbed into or split apart from a continental empire (Europe, China, America or whatever), but one of archipelagic relations, wherein the complexity of anti-nation-state communities create heterogeneous relations among themselves, toward the becoming of a new earth. Therefore, our thought and act are concentrated on the decomposition—rather than even recomposition—of Japan, from within and without.

THESES ON ISLAMISM

"The laws of the physical universe—that the heaven is above earth, that night follows day, etc.—were as much a part of sharia as banning consumption of alcohol and interest on debts. Thus it followed that stars, planets, oceans, rocks, atoms, etc. should actually be considered 'Muslims' since they obey their creator's laws. Rather than Muslims being a minority among humans, one religious group among many, it is non-Muslims who are a small minority among everything in the universe. Of all creatures only humans (and jinn) are endowed with free will, and only non-Muslim humans (and jinn) choose to use that will to disobey the laws of their creator."

—Charles J. Adams

POPULIST IDENTITY

When modern-day Islamism first appeared in the late nineteenth century, it claimed to speak "in the name of a people." This usually meant the invocation of a national or ethnic identity that would coalesce communities of "people" into a larger entity, in order to *move forward* and resist the advances of the West. Islamism was one of the few projects besides communism that could claim to organize in the name of the people, in this case the Islamic *ummah*, or "community," on a truly global scale. It is in this notion of organizing a people, the use of religious identity as a mere instrument, that one finds the origins of the Islamist project. Jamal al-Din al-Afghani, initiator of the modern Islamist project, was himself said to be a Shia from Iran who in turn pretended to be an Afghani, as evinced by his name, in order to project himself as a Sunni. He thus hid his own religious origins and identity in order to reach a wider audience. Whether or not this story is true, it reveals the populist nature of Islamism as it was originally conceived. According to British colonial reports, al-Afghani was not even a practicing Muslim—he did not observe Ramadan, the most basic of Muslim rituals. Al-Afghani saw what the British colonial forces had done in India and was concerned about the same fate befalling the Muslim world, particularly the Qajar (Iranian), Ottoman, and Egyptian empires. He was interested in some kind of supra-identity around which people could organize to allow themselves to resist the military, political, and social advances of the West, while *advancing forward* on their own terms.

One can broadly label this approach "Islamic identitarianism," in that it hinges on the identification of the Muslim subject as a locus of political identity. This form of identitarianism had to later contend with the creation of various nation-states, often pseudo ethno-states, that emerged in the wake of the great wars, specifically the fall of the Ottoman Empire. Thus, Islamic identitarianism could safely identify itself within the confines of the nation-state model and the mechanism of citizenship.

Many go beyond this by advocating an Islamic identity attached to the global ummah outside of the nation-state, often with a sense of the ummah being superior to, or in contradiction with, nationality. These two subjects, Muslim citizen and Muslim believer, have the potential to be, though need not be, contradictory. Islamic identitarianism operates on the same plane as nationalism or fascism. It creates an identitarian form that can cooperate with, reinforce, grate against, or even clash with some notion of citizenship. In this sense, in the Arab world, Islamism can occupy the same place ethno-nationalism does in the West. If whiteness or ethnic identity is the specter in the shadows of liberal democracy, conflating and confusing the idea of what it means to be a citizen, Islamism is the specter of Islam that hovers, some say ominously, over the meaning of being an Arab, a Turk, or a Persian today. This overdetermination is also due to the fact that in much of the Muslim world, the link between ethnicity and citizenship is not ambiguous at all but official, thus transferring the underlying tensions between ethnicity and citizenship to the heart of the state.

POPULIST SPACE

Where Islamism differs markedly from fascism, of course, is in its egalitarian and globalizing disposition, offering a series of explicit counterpoints to Nasserism, Baathism, and Turkish nationalism, as well as other ethnonationalisms with which it finds itself in competition.

One might wonder, then, where is the Left? The Left's failure, in comparison with the Islamists' success, has been analyzed as a result of Cold War defeat and a preference on the part of the United States for Islamism as opposed to the Communist parties or national socialism. It ultimately succumbs to the usual canard of failing to examine the internal dynamics of both Islamist and left projects in the Middle East, and places the fate of both in the hands of Western machinations.

When Arabo-Muslim movements are compared to Islamist ones, this is usually on *ideological* grounds, in order to determine which ones have a *popular ideology*. What is more important to assess, however, is not the question of the *political ideology* at play, but the *space where such a politics* is conducted, and how power is organized within it. The Muslim Brotherhood offers a constructive example. The movement began in Ismailia, the Egyptian headquarters of the Suez Canal, owned by the British and designed and overseen by a group of British as well as French engineers. In the twenties, though Egypt was nominally independent, Egyptians lived under British political, economic, and cultural domination. Nowhere was this more evident than in Ismailia, where British industries operated with impunity on Egyptian soil. As in many other places, British companies underpaid and abused Egyptian workers, and the liberal Wafd Party that ruled Egypt at the time governed impotently, unable to face these challenges. The situation that led to the creation of the Muslim Brotherhood resembles the kind of incident that would have produced a union, workers' cooperative, or a socialist organization. Six workers affiliated with the Suez Canal company approached Hassan al-Banna, a primary school teacher, to complain about British mistreatment, and, soon after, with this teacher as its leader, the Muslim Brotherhood was born.

The Muslim Brotherhood succeeded by building its new community on pre-existing networks, thus utilizing the strength and resilience of old communal forms while creating new ones. Hassan al-Banna himself would of course preach in mosques, but also in modern spaces like cafes, which were frowned upon by the religious establishment. The Muslim Brotherhood would work within already existing networks of Islamic charity and neighborhood associations, pushing these spaces toward a new form of Islamic identity at once local and organic. New recruits did not enter a mass organization, but were placed within units called *usars*, or families. In this way, the group differed from the liberal model of the West, not only in ideological terms, but in the very structure of a new form of political subjectivation. Within less than a decade, the Muslim Brotherhood was more than half a million strong and its support extended well beyond Egypt's borders.

The interplay between embedded structures of communal power and the rupture produced by Islamist ideology is a key element in the Islamist organization of collective power. In Iran in 1979, for example, Islamist activists were able to leverage the power of the longstanding communal networks of bazaars and mosques not only into a strong organization, but one that reconstituted the very nature of the state during the Iranian Revolution.

These grassroots spaces form the *political consistency* of Islamism in more profound ways than the ideology of any given political party, to such an extent that their limits and potentials became those of the Islamist political project itself. In contrast, the global Left, since the second half of the twentieth century, has been deprived of the local forms of worker organization that formed its base and has suffered the consequences. The Left has primarily been constituted by student movements and parties that exist solely to compete for power with the state. When the Left has had any relevance, it has engaged with struggles through similar local forms, for example through the civil rights movement, largely organized by and growing within the struggles of Black churches in the American South.

In the Middle East, the Left has mainly focused its efforts within two spaces, both of which have defined the conditions of struggle. The first is the university—transitory, urban, and an easy target of the state. The second is the state itself, although—in the Arab world especially—it is nothing but an instrument of tyranny and corruption, and the arbitrary use of violence. This led to a fracture, with tyrannical nationalist and Stalinist tendencies on one hand, and groups that risk insignificance on the other. The leftist factions that refuse cooptation by a tyrannical state take refuge in civil society, where they become intertwined with liberal groups and the world of non-governmental organizations, now supported by Western funding and disdained by way of accusations of conspiracy that inevitably follow.

Absent from the mosque—one of the few places one could speak freely—the Left forfeited a crucial space of political and communal organization. In Egypt, Nasser's Bonapartist state sought instead to co-opt agricultural cooperatives and trade unions, leaving the mosque to remain as one of the few untouched spaces for public or communal organization.

EGYPT AND ISLAMISM

Before the Arab Spring of 2011, in much of the Middle East and North Africa the existence and reception of a given political party depended much less on its ideological orientation than its proximity to the ruling regime. In Egypt and Syria, in every ideological tendency from communism to liberalism to Islamism, the true line of separation passed between the parties co-opted by the regime, and the ones that might supposedly share their ideology but remained either illegal or severely restrained, due to the looming threat of state repression. When in 2011 revolution arrived in Egypt, new parties were able to enter the fray, and many of the co-opted parties were unable to compete on their own without regime support.

In Egypt in the seventies an important event occurred that sheds light on the perilous path of the 2011 Egyptian Revolution. During President Sadat's Infitah period,[1] many government services became privatized. As charities and non-governmental organizations picked up the slack, this increased the power and influence of both businessmen and the communal networks of mosques and the Coptic Church. This became particularly important after the Revolution, as certain established political parties lost credibility, and social movements tried to convert themselves into organized parties. In this light, the success of newly created parties like the Freedom and Justice Party of the Muslim Brotherhood movement; the Nour Party coming from the network of the Salafi Call; and the Free Egyptians Party formed through an alliance of the business networks and financial power of billionaire Naguib Sawaris and the Coptic Orthodox Church, can be explained by their position. The previous major left group, Tagammu, was thoroughly co-opted by the state. After the revolution, dissidents within the party went on to form the Democratic Worker's Party, and the Communist Party, which had existed secretly within Tagammu, declared its independence.

These leftist parties, nevertheless, were unable to gain the five thousand signatures needed to officially form a political party, and generally leftist or revolutionary tendencies remained divided and unable to group themselves together. In addition, there were the parties of The Revolution

1. Infitah refers to the period in which President Anwar Sadat privatized Egypt by opening the economy to private capital, reversing the reforms of economic nationalization made under former president Gamal Abdel Nasser.

Continues coalition, a party that attracted a lot of young people and focused on dismantling the security state, as well as political parties that appealed to intellectual circles like the Egyptian Social Democratic Party, formed in the wake of the Revolution. Other tendencies manifested in independent labor unions, agricultural cooperatives, intellectual and cultural clubs and youth movements, but failed to coalesce into a coherent national movement.

While under Hosni Mubarak, Egypt held parliamentary elections with some degree of freedom, the presidential elections of 2012 were essentially the first proper presidential elections since Egypt's liberal experiment before World War II. Whereas the parliamentary elections of 2011 and 2012 were more about grassroots networks, the presidential elections of the summer of 2012 were more of a referendum on Egypt's post-revolutionary national character. The effort of unions to emphasize class divisions, or of youth groups to emphasize the role of the police and security apparatuses, failed to capture the public's imagination. The major divides that did capture this imagination, however, consisted of the oppositions between secularism and Islamism, and being for or against the Revolution. Candidates that took clear stands on these issues came out ahead.

The Islamist candidate representing the Justice and Development Party, Mohammed Morsi, garnered 24.78 percent of the vote in the first round. The clearly secular former prime minister and anti-revolutionary Ahmad Shafiq took 23.66 percent of the vote, and the pro-Revolution but staunchly secular Nasserist candidate Hamdeen Sabahi came in third with 20.72 percent. What is interesting about these results is that neither Shafiq nor Sabahi hailed from parties that performed strongly in the parliamentary elections. Sabahi's Nasserist Dignity Party (Karama) had run in the Democratic Alliance for Egypt electoral coalition, headed by the Muslim Brotherhood's Freedom and Justice Party. Though running on a comparatively progressive platform, the Nasserist party projected a fundamentally Arab Nationalist imagination, thus differing from the Marxists and Communists, although it seemed more significant amidst Egypt's post-revolutionary landscape. What Sabahi did share with the Left, however, was an association with university politics that was difficult to shake, leading people to think he lacked the practical knowledge to lead the whole nation and work at high levels of government. While he did well in major cities like Cairo, Alexandria, and Port Said, he lost disastrously in Upper Egypt, where the anti-Islamist vote amongst key constituencies like the Copts and Sufis was captured by Shafiq. In the end, the divide between secularism and Islamism was easier to mobilize people around than any rhetoric about the Revolution. The two candidates who benefited most from this divide, Morsi and Shafiq, ended up making it to the second round.

Though unequivocally secular in his campaign, Sabahi had attempted to foreground the Revolution itself. He was present on January 25, the very first day, when he was wounded by security forces, and he continued to protest the military when they took the reigns of power after Mubarak fell. Toward the end of 2013, however, not only did he support the military coup against Mohamed Morsi, the former Muslim Brotherhood candidate who was Egypt's first democratically elected president, but also General Abdel Fattah al-Sisi's call on July 26, 2013 for mass demonstrations to give the army a mandate to "crush terrorism" (pro-Morsi protesters). The result was a series of violent crackdowns against Morsi's supporters, including large amounts of members of the Muslim Brotherhood. All of this culminated in the Rabaa Massacre—the biggest massacre in modern Egyptian history—as well as the consolidation of al-Sisi's dictatorship.

SALAFISMS

Here is where the history of Salafism comes in as a growing trend within Islamist movements that have sought to break free of the Islamic institutions that are under the purview of the state. Often incorrectly confused with Wahhabism, Salafism as it has been reinvented at the beginning of the twentieth century is a distinctly modern phenomenon.

A useful case study of the emergent nature of the Salafi movement is found in the story of what came to be called the Revolutionary Salafis. The Salafi Call, the broader movement of modern Salafism in Egypt, began in Alexandria during the seventies and was quietist and gradualist in nature, for the most part eschewing the idea of revolution. In fact, organized Islamists, whether of the Brotherhood or Salafist variety, were not present during the initial days of the Revolution and did not participate in the protests against the military that continued after Mubarak stepped down. Toward the end of 2011, however, a growing group of young Salafists appeared. They believed in street protests, completely distrusted establishment politicians, and believed in Sharia *here and now*. These youth came to be known as the Revolutionary Salafists.

The group formed out of followers of the charismatic Sheikh Salah Abu Ismail. The son of a prominent Muslim Brotherhood member, Sheikh Abu Ismail drifted closer and closer to Salafism, finally leaving the Brotherhood all together sometime before the 2011 protest. He was one of the first Salafis to protest Mubarak, and one of the first leaders to warn of the military takeover in the wake of Mubarak's departure. His followers were often dissatisfied members of the Salafi Call or Muslim Brotherhood, while many others were previously unaffiliated, or drawn from the "Ultras," the football clubs known for clashing with the police. The millenarian quality of his rhetoric and leadership, common in Salafism, can be seen in how many reacted to his speeches. As Al-Miqdad Gamal al-Din notes,

> Abu Ismail differs from the traditional Islamist leaders in all his stances, whether on street protests, major crises, on crucial questions such as the constitution, the presidency and even on Sharia. This is why this man will become a movement himself. His partisans will evolve from simple voters to the bearers of a message and of a project. There will soon be a major betrayal by all the Islamist currents. This will lead to a tsunami in political Islam, toward the explosion of all entities of the past, the Muslim Brotherhood and the Salafi Call. Those who leave will be looking for other groups, representing a new message that is different from anything that exists today.

The Revolutionary Salafists reached out to the working class, which they subsumed under the broader moralistic category of *the oppressed and downtrodden*, for whom they claim to fight. The Revolutionary Salafists bywords were Sharia law and revolution. With regard to Sharia law, they believed it should be implemented completely and uncompromisingly as soon as possible. Revolution, for the Salafists, would not be complete until the military wing of the "deep state," and all the remains of the age of Mubarak, were completely overthrown. This brought them into an odd sort of alliance with sections of the radical leftist youth. In fact, the Revolutionary Salafists, along with some of the April 6th Youth Movement, were among the last people still protesting the military in the run-up to the spring 2012 elections.

When Sheikh Abu Ismail submitted his candidacy, he received over one hundred and fifty thousand signatures—more than any other candidate—and was projected to lead round one of the election. His candidacy was cut short, however, by the unexpected revelation that his mother was actually a U.S. citizen. The Revolutionary Salafist movement, built around the figure of this Sheikh, struggled to give itself an institutional existence in his absence, but the group Ahrar (Freedom), one of its offshoots, maintained its own separate identity. As a youth movement, Ahrar emerged with a preference for political action in the street as opposed to the institutional dynamics of political parties. The group violently clashed with the police, preached its message through hymns sung in the style of football chants, appropriated the iconography of the Anonymous movement, including the V for Vendetta mask, and managed to find its way into the universities. During Morsi's presidency, though they were critical of him, many formerly revolutionary Salafists defended him against the liberal and pro-military forces that would unite against him a year later. Ahrar was perhaps the only Islamist movement that continued protesting both against Morsi and against the military, maintaining what they referred to as their "third way."

By way of the first split between Revolutionary Salafists and the Salafist Call, and then later Ahrar from the rest of the Revolutionary Salafists, one can see the dynamism of Salafism through how its vocabulary and ideology continually breaks away from older trends, shedding previous forms of itself now deemed too compromising or inauthentic, and thus constantly positioning itself at the forefront of Islamist politics and populist politics in a more general sense.

Salafism is on the rise everywhere, offering an alternative to classical identitarian Islamism as well as to the elites of state power. Its rise is tied to an antagonistic relationship to mainstream Islamic powers associated with the state, as new Salafist groups or tendencies are created when and where previous ones seemed too conciliatory. The power of Salafism resides in part in its ability to redefine a new cosmology of which politics is only one mere facet and not an end, in contrast with communism, liberalism and nationalism. Salafism can place itself in direct opposition to established religious and political hierarchies, appealing directly to a specific religious community of like-minded people for its legitimacy.

In a seemingly contradictory manner, modern day Salafism grew out of the Islamic modernism of Jamal al-Din al-Afghani and his Egyptian student, Muhammad Abduh, the father of what could be called "Islamic Liberalism." Whereas al-Afghani sought a pan-Islamism to unite Muslim peoples and civilizations against the forces of Western colonialism, Abduh sought to discard much of the ossified schools of thought that had come to be associated with Islamic interpretation. He did this in order to uncover a "true Islam," which he believed would correspond closely to modern reason and rationality. In short, his interpretation of Islam went against the traditional established doctrines, making a space for an Islam that could be more modern and rational on the one hand, but also more unexpectedly doctrinaire and puritanical on the other. The tendencies between a more liberal and a more fanatic Islam would grow more distinct as modern Islamism took shape in the twentieth century, defined by this duplicity between rationalism and puritanism. Modern Salafism's liberation of religious interpretation from the hierarchies of power and interpretative authority bring to mind early Protestantism, which also possessed an authentic religious fervor, fanaticism, and a certain populist emancipatory potential.

Muhammed Rashid Rida (1865–1935) provided the missing link between al-Afghani and Abduh's early liberal Islamism and modern Salafism as we know it. Born in the Ottoman Empire in present-day Lebanon, Rashid Rida's desire to restore Islam to its original form was coupled by a deep distrust toward traditional bastions of power: the established Sufi orders and the Grand Muftis, or the officially sanctioned religious academies. This distrust led him to center his philosophy on creating or accessing a direct link between the community of believers and the will of God, as mediated by the Quran, thus reconfiguring Islamic ideas of piety, dignity, and meaning. This remained a central theme for the Salafist thinkers who succeeded him. Again, much like early Protestantism, many schools of Salafism emerged around different leaders, who sought to restore a true Islam and fulfill a religious destiny. Martin Luther and the early Protestants also addressed the People directly, opening up a space for a direct relationship between the individual or congregation and the Bible, away from the mediation of the corrupt Catholic Church and the arbitrary power of oppressive monarchical forces. In this sense, Salafism is very much a popularization of the moral universe. However, much like Protestant puritanism, Salafism abolishes or attempts to undermine the "earthly power" of rulers by embracing piety—a traditional marker of respect and power—and raising it above all other qualities. The benchmark for piety then becomes not the ruling of a certain jurist or school, but the conduct of the Prophet Muhammad himself as revealed in the *Hadith*, a collection of the Prophet's proverbs and deeds, sayings and doings. In this creation of a single standard for piety not tied to the juridical power of larger Islamic institutions, much less institutions of the state, Salafism establishes a kind of puritanical form of egalitarianism.

TO GO BEYOND

Beyond Salafism, Islamism generally can rearticulate life away from the material plane to a metaphysical reality where the oppressed are empowered, and receive courage and the capacity to act. Populist politics is present all over the Arab world. Whether it's Arab ethnonationalism, the nationalist Islamism of the Muslim Brotherhood, Salafism, or the internationalist populism of the jihadists, it often entails an appeal and symbolic gesture toward a God and his People—these people who are his field of action on which to enact truth. This highly moralistic and mystical character of populism is a failed attempt to grasp something much broader: a need, a desire, and a struggle in the Arab world for what could be called a *politics of dignity*.

The Arab Spring was as much about dignity as material poverty. In Tunisia, the street vendor Mohamed Bouazizi was protesting a form of injustice so deep that it penetrated the core of his very being. The annihilation of his flesh became the only way to negate it. It is not just the question of poverty, as there are far more impoverished places in the world. It was a cosmic sense of injustice felt by Bouazizi, and felt amongst the poor, that animated the movement.

The struggle is not so much between the rich and the poor, but between the powerful and the uncounted. Islamist politics addresses this lack of dignity much more profoundly than secular policies have been able to. There is a scene from the film *We Were Communists* (2010) by Maher Abi Samra, in which an old Communist reflects on how Hezbollah replaced much of the Left in southern Lebanon. He speaks about the first time he was called *Sayyed*, an Islamic honorific signifying "descendant of the Prophet." He accounts how different it felt from being called comrade, or even from being called friend. It meant something more, something that evoked a transcendent force. It meant being part of a temporal trajectory and a community that had long preceded him and would long outlast him.

To understand all this, one must understand the logic of authoritarianism and totalitarianism that exists in almost every single Arab country. One must also understand the humiliation and abjection that "citizens" are subjected to at the hands of the powerful and, even more systematically and brutally, at the hands of the state. This arbitrary application of power creates a craving for a rule anchored in that which is beyond the ephemeral whims of humanity. The corrupt utilization of the law as a tool sullies the idea of secular law. The transcendent nature of religious law, which gains its legitimacy from beyond the state, is more important than the content of the law itself.

Torture, humiliation, and sexual violence in particular create a yearning for a social form that could transcend such a system. For example, if one is arrested by the police during a protest, it is *as a citizen* that one is tortured by the police. If the honor of one's family member is violated, *as a citizen*, then it is vital to be something other than citizen in order to fight for a different sort of relation among humans. This is why the populist argument against the idea of a civil state gains traction amongst hardline Islamists, and for those for whom the term *citizen* has become irrevocably soiled.

In a 2016 speech, Syrian leader Bashar al-Assad himself said being Syrian was not about having a passport, but about fighting for Syria. By this he meant that Syria didn't belong to its citizens: not those who fled the war and were living as refugees, nor those his government bombed, but those within Syria and from other countries near and far who had come to fight for his government or the status quo it represents. Similar to the ideology of ISIS, Assad meant Syria doesn't belong to its citizens *de facto*, but to those who fight or are loyal to a certain idea, whether this is the mythical caliphate or the state's tyranny. Here the idea of citizenship collapses, and rather than contextualize these dreams in terms of the nation-state model they claim to represent, hardline Islamism attempts to reconfigure the battlefield.

During the Syrian insurrection, sexual violence and torture was used to incite people. The Revolution began in Daraa, a province in southern Syria where a number of school children were abducted by state security for scribbling "The People want the fall of the regime" on the wall. When the families went to the authorities in Daraa to inquire about their children, a high-ranking bureaucrat told them: "Forget about those kids. Send me your wives, I'll help you make some new ones." Such a statement essentially represents the confluence of class, power, sex, family, personal honor, and the indignity that drives people toward ever more uncompromising versions of Islamism. Later, during protests against these same school children's detainment, another boy named Hamza Ali al-Khateeb was arrested, detained, and returned to his parents as a tortured and sexually mutilated corpse. Though the movement was still largely non-Islamist, this moment is precisely when the protests began turning violent. It is not widely understood how much torture and sexual humiliation—either of oneself or one's family member—drove people toward armed groups, and especially those with a Salafi mindset, later on during the war. To be abducted by the state, or to have a friend, neighbor, or family member abducted or victimized by the state, is to experience the most extreme form of powerlessness. To fight such a powerlessness, one could only renounce oneself to a much more powerful cosmology.

The current war in Syria, and the slaughter being carried out by the regime of Assad and his allies, is made possible by the confluence of two trajectories: profound inequalities between social classes and a certain form of Islamophobia. The parts of Syria that are being cleansed today are those that rose up or continue to rise up against Assad's rule, but are also the areas of the *undesirables*. Individuals of all religious, ethnic, and class backgrounds protested and fought against the regime, but it is no coincidence that the communities that took up arms and were thus besieged, starved, and bombed to dust were predominantly composed of the Sunni working class. The decimated areas around Homs, Aleppo, and Damascus were almost invariably the poor Sunni-majority sections of towns. These residents' flight has allowed the regime and the ruling class that stood with it to engage in construction projects and economic development: ethnic cleansing becomes a tool of gentrification.

There is, within the Arab world, a deep fear of the Muslim, and in particular the Sunni Muslim, who forms the "mass" of the people. This fear of the angry masses of Sunnis, and in particular of the Sunni Islamism epitomized by the Salafist movement, is found amongst the rich as well as minority communities. In the counter-revolutionary backlash to the 2011 uprising, these two have converged more than ever.

POPULIST SOVEREIGNTY AND ITS NEGATION

While Islamic identitarianism primarily seeks to identify as Islamic, Islamic fundamentalism grounds itself in an empirical reality: the existence of God and the divinity of the holy Quran, with all politics necessarily flowing from there. Nowhere can the gulf between identitarianism and fundamentalism be seen more clearly seen than in the debates sparked around the creation of the Pakistani state in 1947. The separation of Pakistan from the rest of India came out of the worldview of organisms like the All India Muslim League. The idea was that Muslims and Hindus within India constituted two separate nations, and thus Muslims deserved their own nation. These efforts were not met with universal acclaim by Islamists, many of whom juxtaposed the idea of a "Muslim Nation" against the struggle for an actual "Islamic State" that would strive to implement God's will. In doing so, they foregrounded God as the sovereign as opposed to Muslim subjects or rulers. This was the position of one of the intellectual pioneers of Islamic fundamentalism, Abul A'la Maududi, who founded the Jamaat-e-Islami as a third way between the All India Muslim League, which pushed for creation of Pakistan, and the Indian National Congress, which sought to maintain a united India. The position of Jamaat-e-Islami, under the leadership of Abul A'la Maududi, was that "an Islamic state is a Muslim state, but a Muslim state may not be an Islamic state unless and until the Constitution of the state is based on the Qur'an and Sunnah."

For the fundamentalist, God acts in the human world not by way of individual belief, but through the ways humans relate to one another within society, and how these relations are inscribed in the state. The central mechanism of this is Sharia, which means the "way" and can be understood as a corpus of laws that should govern the human world. In this context, the Quran is not just a book to turn to for wisdom or guidance, but a model for social relations as the infallible word of God. Living as humans together within Islam is more important than what any individual actually believes. In a pure Islamic fundamentalist view, the root of the problem is human intentionality itself. This intentionality seeks to gaze upon, subdue and enslave all within its purview. Since nature itself is already entirely subservient to God and his laws (in this sense nature is already Muslim), studying natural laws is studying divine law. Thus to submit to divine law is to find one's place within nature. As Sayyid Qutb, one of the major fundamentalist thinkers, notes:

> Islam teaches that God created the physical world and all its forces for man's own use and benefit. Man is specifically taught and directed to study the world around him, discover its potential and utilize all his environment for his own good and the good of his fellow humans. Any harm that man suffers at the hands of nature is a result only of his ignorance or lack of understanding of it and of the laws governing it. The more man learns about nature, the more peaceful and harmonious his relationship with nature and the environment. Hence, the notion of "conquering nature" can readily be seen as cynical and negative. It is alien to Islamic perceptions and betrays a shameless ignorance of the spirit in which the world has been created and the divine wisdom that underlies it.

The writings of Islamist fundamentalists are replete with descriptions of the state as a collection and organization of brute power, arbitrarily exercised and all-encompassing in nature. Nowhere is this truer than in the writings of Qutb, a philosopher, poet and former leader of the Muslim Brotherhood who was detained in 1954 for helping plot the assassination of former Egyptian leader Gamal Abdel Nasser. Qutb was imprisoned without a proper trial, tortured, and humiliated. It was in his jail cell, stripped of all power over his own body and completely at the mercy of the penal machine, where he composed two of the most important works of Islamic fundamentalist thought: *In the Shade of the Quran* and *Milestones*. In both works, he outlines the two concepts of *al-'ubudiyya* and *al-hakimiyya*. While *al-'ubudiyya* is willing submission to the rules of God, *al-hakimiyya* is acknowledging His supremacy. The relation between the two concepts goes back to human intentionality and the problems it creates. *Al-'ubadiyya* states that willful obedience precedes individual belief. True belief can only form itself through a humble engagement with the reality of the miraculous divine, and thus human will should be guided by submission to *al-hakimmiya*, rather than intentionality. Since nature is already subservient to the will of God, and humans are divided from nature because of their free will, it is only by their *willful* obedience to God that they rejoin the rest of the universe. Indeed, a will merely guided by intention, divorced from obedience to the majestic, can only be a will to enslave and destroy not only other men, but nature itself.

When we consider Islamism as a political project in continuity with the other great ideologies of the twentieth century, the particularity of Islamic fundamentalism theoretically lies in its desire to immediately do away with the tyranny of men (dictatorship), of the masses (democracy), of greed (capitalism), and authoritarian bureaucracy (the modern state). To locate sovereignty within the human dialectically entails the necessity of slavery and subjection, since slavery and subjection can only exist as a form of human relation. In the nineteenth and twentieth centuries, different ideologies have deployed the locus of the sovereign to call into question a problem of time immemorial: the problem of human domination. The way to eliminate it is by eliminating human sovereignty itself. This is done by placing it beyond rulers, nations, and classes, even beyond religion—by placing it in the hands of the Divine. In this sense, for fundamentalists, sovereignty is no longer a human problem.

In this way, fundamentalism seeks to dismantle the state, not to reform it for its own sake, but to reconstitute it as an instrument of the Divine. In seeking to do so, Islamic fundamentalists address the human community directly, and not only the instrument of the state. The state is now seen as a repository, the accumulation and crystallization of the alienated and aggressive human intentions. In such a world, there would be no need for police, as laws would not need to be enforced because the future human would willingly submit to them. There would also ultimately be no rulers. In Qutb's reading of the Quran, with a properly advanced community of willing believers, there would be no need for further arbitration. No longer a government nor governed, only a community of believers without mediation, save that of the Quran itself. In this way, Qutb reveals the utopic and nihilistic nature of Islamic fundamentalism.

Short-circuiting classical politics, he develops a politics in the name of a meta-people—the *ummah*. This involves the creation of new communities of willful believers through preaching, but also the destruction of *al-Jahiliyyah*, taken to mean the social, political and economic structures of oppression, degeneracy, and ignorance that characterize the present world. The struggle to destroy *al-Jahiliyyah* is what is referred to as jihad.

POPULIST ISLAM

There is nothing inevitable in the Arab or Muslim world. Nothing determines this drift toward Islamist hegemony. The crucial question for the forces that constitute an alternative is how to not dismiss Islamist movements while also avoiding a fall into their logic. It is not about relating to Islamists as a *fait accompli*, but asking the more tactically and ethically important question of *why Islamists are the way they are*. To do as the Islamist without being as the Islamist is not to ask how to impose a popular imaginary, but how to build off and adapt to what exists, how to put into place not only the most powerful form of organization, but one that would be able to proliferate at the most local level. And when the time comes, most importantly, how to command a level of self-sacrifice that doesn't lead to a pure and simple annihilation.

Nationalists, liberals, and leftists have lost connection to the humans in whose name they claim to speak. In the name of Syrian nationalism, Assad destroys Syria. The leftists, Syrians, and Arab nationalists who support him claim his annihilation is necessary for the "Syrian People." The states that defend the Palestinian cause care nothing for Palestinians themselves. In Lebanon, the notion that Palestinian refugees have a right to return is used both by the state and the Palestinian factions themselves as an excuse to deny the refugees a life of dignity. This is the predicament of the Arab world, disavowing an investment in bettering life in the here and now in the name of that over which one has no power or actively betrays. Arabism, Islam, and anti-imperialism have today become totems, alienated and instrumentalized symbols to subjugate those in whose name they claim to act: the mythical triumph of a working class, the unification of the Arab world, the defeat of Israel, etc. The contradiction, then, is between Syria and actual Syrians, the

Palestinian cause and Palestinians, the working class and the Left, liberalism and human dignity.

In this abyss between causes and beings, Islamism grows, slowly but surely, to constitute a political project. The Islamists take no shame in saying the cause of Islam is greater than Muslims, because the profound truth of Islam must overwhelm the reality of mere Muslim life.

The only way to counter Islamist logic is to reconcile the human with its different causes: the hopes and aspirations of Egyptians with Egypt as a reality and a territory, the dignity of the working class with the revolution, the well-being and autonomy of Arab women against the feminism that speaks in their name. In short, to repair the existential contradictions that are tearing our world apart.

AMERICAN TRIPTYCH

This text is a triptych on the United States. It presents three distinct lines of thought that nevertheless echo and intersect, intertwining different times in an articulation that is the beginning of another history, and thus, of another possible present...

SONS OF LIBERTY

1

The disavowal of America has been manufactured by Americans, endowing the national identity with a simplicity and ease embraced by both its patriots and opponents. This denial has produced an impoverishment in self-conception, directly alongside the country's unprecedented acquisition of material wealth.

The risk of those who rebel has been to lose themselves in the fantasy that to overthrow America begins by pretending it doesn't exist—that it never existed. The narratives projected upon America both from within and without have always been fantasy, but consciously so. To speak about power has always been to speak sideways, through anecdote, story, invocation. But even the most fanatical should humbly pause in consideration of exactly what has taken place within a few hundred years on this continent. To undo and overcome such an entrenched force requires some acknowledgement and understanding, some patience.

Those who find themselves struggling against the United States today too often stumble from the misconception that a revolutionary force is solely a question of invention, rather than a rearticulation and reassemblage of what already exists—of what may have always existed. The question of beginning again would not be one of invention and imagination, but rather of a sensitivity to our given and historical realities—to the materials around us. Ours is not a struggle of producing identity, but of an allegiance to narrative truth. This is our impossible beginning: these places, their peoples, their myths and histories, everything that can be made into a memory—where political victory is bound with the capacity to tell a better story.

If disintegration, disarticulation, and disaggregation are the figures of the present—for us and the millions whose atomization we share—the dominant myth of America and its western frontier persists. Just as the Occident operates within the global imaginary, so too does *the West* within America:

it is less of a place and more of an orientation. The myth of the American remains one of reinvention: the pioneers of the New World encountering a space wherein they could reimagine who they were and what they could be, animated by the promise of a new life freed from a dismal past. As with all settler-colonial projects, to confront their simultaneously utopian and apocalyptic imaginaries is to face what has always been *revolutionary* within these state processes of subjectivization. The question of revolution in America today is not the overthrowing of a state apparatus as it presently discloses itself, but rather a wresting away of that revolutionary character with which it self-defines.

We must now identify whether the present configuration of forces is distinct. If the United States was a product and result of a wave of revolutions within England and France, it is also the vanguard of imagining what a decomposition of their liberal project might look like: rampant individualism and self-reliance, distrust of institutions, the embrace of conspiracy, and the push for furthering both personal and national isolationism. If Donald Trump's presidency signals the failure of the American political system, its truth also signals that same collapse taking place globally. The shipwreck of the United States is that of a vision of the world. As Franz Rosenzweig said in 1919, "when a world collapses, the ideas to which it gave birth, the dreams that passed through it, also vanish under the ruins." Rosenzweig bitterly observed the remains of European imperial dreams at the same moment when, on the other side of the Atlantic, with Ford, a new world affirmed its universality, filled with the same promises that sink today.

Faced with no other way forward, we contend with unfortunate fantasies both romantic and desperate: the demand for an impossible "new" New Deal, the cartoonish street and virtual encounters of middle-class fascists and antifascist youth, the Far Right's invocation of civil war. While such an implosion was aspired to for decades as an opportunity, its current form portends increased widespread misery, combined with continued authoritarianism and oppression. We might now look to those who have organized themselves for survival across time. To begin is to make sense of the remnants, of all we've seen and heard coming of age in this place, in what has become a seductive oblivion of appearances.

2

Impoverishment constructs binaries—false antinomies—to flatten and deaden the world. Taking place within every terrain, this opposition exists within politics between electoral representation on the one hand and the grassroots social movement on the other. If the progression of history revolves around a series of crises—and movements, proposals, and decisions in response—this would take hold both within the dominant institutions of governance as well as the popular and spontaneous experiments outside of them. Both create narratives that lay claim to legitimacy and authenticity, presenting an experience of truth within their frameworks of engagement and participation. Within both the People are simultaneously present and alienated, committed materially yet abstracted in essence. Both include dynamics of passivity and action, collectivity and individuality, but neither a nihilist nor voluntarist tactical orientation approaches real engagement with the presently functioning forms of power. This is not a question of a particular protest or occupation, nor candidate nor election, but rather a survey of the ways each of these can represent a sentiment and base to which we feel drawn—to have a potential to change narratives and expectations around both politics and life, and therefore of a future.

In response to the 2007–2008 financial crisis, two distinct waves of popular protest mobilized in the United States. Both the Tea Party and Occupy Wall Street assembled their roots, aesthetics, tactics, and discourses from the national political life of America, though their precise modes of articulation were distinct. Today's populisms become legible only within a broader context of overdetermination and collapse. Constant repetitions speak of generalized crisis and exclusion, of environmental devastation and displacement, and of a social and spiritual collapse whose names and forms are too numerous to elaborate. Everywhere chaos appears it is the People, in both their nostalgic and futurist modes, who are to restore order and sense. These recent movements in America—in their right, left, and blurred variations—were socialized articulations against the governmental ordering of the present. They unleashed a living assemblage of ideas, behaviors, memories, slogans, and semiotic fragments that, once aggregated, took on a magnetism. Their formalizations were necessarily ambiguous and unstable. The populist movement struggles to institute a consistency while simultaneously resisting the external application of an ordering truth.

The Tea Party's rise was a reaction to the presidencies of both Barack Obama and George W. Bush—an opportunity to decisively break with their institutional visions and the parties they led, and to embrace the return of right populism to American national politics in the form of libertarian nativism. The movement's harkening to the Boston Tea Party of 1773 placed it in the lineage of America's revolutionary mythology. In that year, the Sons of Liberty, a conspiratorial society of artisans, merchants, and lawyers, attacked and destroyed an English tea shipment in protest of excessive taxes and other grievances against the British Empire. Beyond the perpetual demand for lower taxes, the contemporary lives of a large number of middle-class Americans—for whom the Tea Party movement offered a departure from suburban isolation and a *form* to voice their rage—would appear to share little with their historical counterparts. Yet all this frames the contemporary movement's attire in revolutionary and patriotic costumes and masks, simultaneously celebrating and distorting the legacy of the farmers and traders who triumphed against the British in the guerilla warfare that birthed a nation.

According to a central organizer of the Tea Party Patriots, just one of its many factions, the Tea Party movement stood broadly and vaguely for "lower taxation, smaller government, and adherence to the United States Constitution." State governments' reliance on property tax incomes in an age of austerity helped create the economic pressures that would become the source of both the radicalization and decomposition of the American middle class. Caught in the conflicted promises of their American dream, today's middle-class partisans wished to unfetter an economy whose brutal reign has been destroying the comforts of their contracting way of life. This combination of cosmology and collectivity was an early index of the increasingly bizarre sanatorium that became political life in America. Respectable adults and families appeared on the unpeopled corners of lifeless suburban trafficways to engage in what seemed like a theater of the avant-garde—men dressed in colonial cocked hats, ruffles, and breaches, while others wore tea bags dangling off of baseball caps.

Appropriately, the movement began on television. Though the term had been used by the followers of former Texas congressman Ron Paul, the name

Tea Party passed a threshold of formalization in February 2009 during a rant by Rick Santelli, a hedge fund manager turned cable business news editor. Incensed that then president Barack Obama would suggest subsidizing the "losers' mortgages" in the wake of the subprime mortgage crisis, Santelli's live-broadcasted rant at the Chicago Stock Exchange bemoaned government expenditure on behalf of the *irresponsible*, and was welcomed with cheers from brokers on the trading room floor. Santelli depicts his upper-middle class as a *typical people*: "These guys are pretty straightforward, and my guess is, a pretty good statistical cross-section of America, the silent majority." He closes with a feverish demand to found a new Tea Party, one that would rise up against Obama's left tyranny. The portrayal of the president as a socialist anticapitalist is a testament to the country's long rightward march, and the casting of liberals as extremists is a recurrent motif within the last century's right populism. Contained in Santelli's speech is an enduring and dominant figure of populism, that of the *two-way fight*—any given struggle oriented toward both a big enemy and a little enemy. While the enduring target of mainstream conservatism remains the apparent differences in identity and culture of the little enemy—sexual, religious, linguistic, and ethnic—right populism's big enemy is an elusive composite imaginary of globalist machinations and a distended state apparatus. Both mobilize conspiratorial, paranoid, and survivalist rhetoric to justify their worldview and resulting proposals for a future.

To place the Tea Party and Occupy Wall Street side by side is to measure their opportunities for engagement and truth as a horizon for life in America. They offered frameworks of response to the structural uncertainties of the nation, and counted on a commitment and decision that their public visibility and popular diffusion represent a singular political rupture. Both emphasized decentralization in their appearance as localized manifestations of a shared sentiment, rather than a nationally coordinated institutional expression. Both emphasized independence from America's political party system, and more broadly from any pre-existing political organization. This was all characteristic of the global upheavals which spread throughout 2011, from the Arab Spring to the plaza occupations along the Mediterranean in Europe. These spontaneous assemblages in the streets and plazas were endlessly seductive and inspiring—their experiments with new forms of encounter and association were a hopeful imaginary for a new political body and global movement that no longer saw itself represented within contemporary classical politics.

From our experiences and memories of the Tea Party and Occupy Wall Street, there were no particular individuals around whom the movements' narratives might be reduced. They were the movements of a time, which was both their strength and limitation. As their contagion, enthusiasm, and optimism waned, larger personalities, institutions, and agendas preyed upon them to suck up their energies, talents, and potentials. This was not simply a defeat or recuperation, but an inevitability. A politics of time is necessarily won with stamina, with duration—the victors are those best positioned to train within that arena. If grassroots social movements have ebbed and flowed in interest, popularity, and potency within America, representative democratic governance has continued essentially unchallenged. As the Tea Party and Occupy Wall Street faded in both intensity and memory, what they hinted at was to be absorbed in the electoral process—another form of measurement of whether their public demonstrations could resonate nationally. As the rhetoric and platform of Occupy Wall Street would find itself reflected and generalized in the 2016 campaign of Vermont senator Bernie Sanders, so too did the Tea Party lay the groundwork for the presidential candidacy and victory of Donald Trump. The combination of popular frustration and impotence in the wake of governmental failure led directly to the fervor witnessed in the 2016 presidential election and its debates. The lingering question is whether these movements and campaigns were in fact always competing for the same audience, the same people, the same potentialities.

The United States' 2016 election revealed the depths of the contemporary crisis of representation, taking place both nationally and globally. America's two main parties' ability to absorb both internal dissent and grassroots social movements is the measure of their capacity to steer political possibility in the country. The expected contest pitting the presidential dynasties of the Bush and Clinton families against each other turned into a free-for-all of polarizing personalities like Texas senator Ted Cruz and real estate mogul Donald Trump on the one side, and Bernie Sanders, an independent, self-identified "democratic socialist," on the other. The Tea Party marked an insurgency within the Republican Party, altering its discourse and infusing its ranks by way of local electoral victories that cleared the path for Trumpian nihilism. Governmental and institutional realities that had long been taken for granted as the basis of post-war reality—the North American Free Trade Agreement (NAFTA), the Trans-Pacific Partnership (TPP), the North Atlantic Treaty Organization (NATO), and the Central Intelligence Agency (CIA)—were now vulnerable targets to be attacked from both the right and left on a national stage, and Americans were surprisingly excited. The Sanders-Clinton primary and Trump's victory represented a catastrophe for their respective parties, existentially questioning whether they continue to function as coherent organizations developing and pushing a national agenda, or if they have simply become bloated and symbolic institutional receptacles for movements organized independently.

What has been at stake is whether those left out of the American political machine—the parties, the elections, the economy—can self-organize to manifest into a social force. Or, whether the political apparatus has strengthened itself enough to successfully cast off an ever-growing amount of people without work, hope, or any sense of meaningful social participation in the machinations of the state. The Far Left has wagered everything on this representation-less mass—a self-perpetuating imaginary of a new political subject to organize around, after having been ousted from politics. As the country's grassroots social movements ran out of energy and space, they were unable to envision the forms of alliance, organization, and stamina to withstand those formations better composed and constituted. From Bashar al-Assad to Donald Trump, this is the present we find ourselves in today.

3

Within the United States, populism has less to do with policy than it does the subjective construction of the American. This is the primary domain of governance in the United States, and the competing narratives within the nation revolve around Americans' mutual self-definitions and the resulting expectations and requirements of their conclusions. U.S. history has produced a series of subjectivities elevated into representative supremacy: the settler, the colonist, the plantation owner, the Protestant revivalist, the patriot revolutionary, the republican federalist, the pioneer frontiersman, the Unionist, the African American citizen, the industrialist, the laborer, the Catholic, the segregationist, the Progressive, the migrant, the nativist, the Prohibitionist, the suffragette flapper, the consumer, the struggling farmer, the liberal New Dealer, the democratic capitalist, the feminist, the conservative Reaganite, the neoconservative, etc. The hegemonic American subject was and remains constantly shifting, in conflict and in contradiction with those identities that came before, as well as those still to come.

Political opposition in the United States is the struggle for either the domination or integration of external and hostile identities into the American political process: the Indian, the Brit, the slave, the Loyalist, the monarchist aristocrat, the woman, the Confederate, the white supremacist, the immigrant, the banker, the Bolshevik, the anarchist, the Soviet, the male chauvinist, the hippie, the terrorist. It's within this framework that we can view American governance through its recuperative narrative of "civil rights." The self-named civil rights movement of African Americans in the fifties and sixties, with the gospel song "We Shall Overcome" as its anthem, made famous this struggle for the full integration into the institutions of American society, wherein the individual citizen or legal resident is given the expectation of legal and social protection. Within the United States, "human rights" remains an external phenomenon that occurs elsewhere, outside of its borders, for and by those outside its jurisdiction. The remaining paradigm of political identification and therefore struggle is that of sovereignty, of true self-rule, which in the United States' history has been tied directly to war, waged against Indigenous peoples and nations resisting European colonization and American state formation; against the British Empire for national independence; and against the Confederate States of America to preserve one unified vision of what it is to be American.

One of the most notorious governmental bodies to preserve this singular vision arose during the so-called "Red Scare," and gave itself the name of the House Un-American Activities Committee (1938–1969). Its titular framing wasn't a reference to the competition of communism versus capitalism as an ideology or system of governance, but rather its mission was precisely concerned with what it meant to be American. After World War II, one of its primary targets of investigation was all those working in Hollywood and the entertainment industries, including actors, directors, musicians, playwrights, radio commentators, and screenwriters. The House Un-American Activities

Committee was not just after Soviet spies and Communist Party functionaries, but those in America with the imagination and spirit to create a new narrative of life: storytellers. Throughout the fifties, hundreds of artists and intellectuals would be blacklisted, unable to find work for no other reason than their political beliefs were deemed "Un-American."

In the United States' largest metropolis, New York City—where we live, where we are from, and where we find ourselves—close to three million people, around forty percent of the population, are born outside of the country. America's population includes more than forty-six million "foreign-born" residents, by far the highest total of any nation in the world. What Americans share is neither religion, nor culture, nor language, nor history, nor citizenship, nor proximity, but solely the process of becoming American.

The European colonization of this continent was not just the settling of its lands and the displacement of its original inhabitants—state formation in the United States included as well the colonization of those still to come and, by extension, the colonization of where they would come from. The United States' population of 325 million represents just four percent of the world's population, but it is the largest consumer economy in the world, with more than a quarter of the global market—larger than the entire European Union. Over the course of the twentieth century, it became clear that the production of Americans was not just a domestic but a global project. The United States and its residents send more remittances abroad than any other country in the world: America's local economy becomes the global economy, as its people become the people of the world.

The displacements discovered within colonization, immigration, enslavement, and urbanization were not just disastrous because of their violent brutality and the material dispossession that resulted, but because of the enduring subjective confusion with which they were bound. We have been cut off by oceans and rivers from where we came from, what we left behind, what we remembered.

The settlers of America maintain no memories of discovery, only of construction. All of those identities, present and competing, have become the demonstration of dispersal. Not as a mode of state repression, but of our inability to become other within an image of our own construction. Those who find themselves in its cities and territories do so already from a space and world of defeat—their domination is no longer that of an individual or state, but of a history. A history we have increasingly lost the capacity to access and understand. The question of America remains one of discovery, but no longer of the place itself, but of what it means to truly inhabit it, of what it means to live here together.

This place is a Tower of Babel in reverse: instead of a unified humanity coming together for a shared construction, we find ourselves here after already having been dispersed, still unable to communicate, but with an architecture already constructed, and not in the way we had imagined. We now have to make sense of these millions of languages, histories, memories, and experiences we and our families have carried here. Of all those who existed in this place before we arrived. And we must put them to use to build our own process of overcoming. All of those travelers and explorers stranded and left behind, of those who never wanted to come, now needing to construct a new ship from the wreckage.

THE PEOPLE OF FORD

"There are countries where a power, in a way external to the social body, acts on it and forces it to follow a certain path. There are others where force is divided, being simultaneously inside and outside the society. Nothing of the sort is seen in the United States; there society acts by itself and on itself. Power exists only inside it; hardly anyone may even be found who dares to conceive and especially to express the idea of seeking power elsewhere."

—Alexis de Tocqueville, *Democracy in America*

When Tocqueville visited the United States in 1831, he noted this new country's mythological vigor. If U.S. "society acts by itself and on itself," it's because its different components are each animated by the same dream. This dream consisted of the endless conquest of a liberty without borders, the primary bond unifying the men of the new world. Yet liberty only functions by way of infinity, in distinguishing the interior limit from the exterior. Every limit must abolish itself in liberty's name: American Indians, slavery, borders, nature, etc. Such is the matrix of the American dream. This dream soon became a nightmare in 1913, however, when the first automated assembly lines arrived in Ford's factories. Or again in 1917 when the United States went to war. Praising the *Gospel of Work*, innumerable immigrant masses had to become "the American people," only to return and die on the banks of the Old World. What Henry Ford inaugurated was not only a new form of work—and thus worker, relation between commandment and worker, and thus finally commandment—but also a new populist problematic. How does one produce a culturally homogenous artifact of something "American" out of all these Poles, Russians, Italians, Sicilians, Romanians, Austrians, and Hungarians? How does one make them loyal to a homeland and to the promise of the American Dream, whose realization finally depends on the people's loyalty to itself? In other words, how does one make this heap of differentiated ethnicities understand that they themselves are *America*?

In Detroit, in fact, such loyalty was largely in question. In 1913—the same year as the Ludlow Massacre—ten percent of Ford's 13,000 workers in Highland Park were absent every day, and yearly turnover was around 350 percent. In response, Ford inaugurated the highest worker salary in the United States. While at five dollars per day his workers became the highest-paid in the world, the salary didn't come without a price. At the end of the workday, the immigrant worker received two dollars and fifty cents. The other half was a "profit" he received provided he responded to certain productive, moral, and hygienic standards. Directed by an emblematic figure named S.S. Marquis, the Ford Sociological Department was tasked with making moral inquiries into the workers in order to separate the good from the bad. The firm's Americanization program also created the Ford English School. According to S.S. Marquis, the school, based on the image of the Model T assembly line, had to be able to engineer a calibrated human product stamped *American* upon completion. "The first thing we teach them to say is 'I'm a good American,' and then we try to make them live according to this statement." The school was bursting with such stupid statements that students had to learn, and which can still be found today in English language textbooks. In reality, what Ford's students learned was the language of consumption—this booming new social relation—and also linguistic codes of English politeness, decorum, and Puritan morality. The student even had the opportunity to walk in the coveted shoes of an American who goes to the bank, saves, buys various cultural and other artifacts, argues with his wife, or even invites his neighbors to his house. The values of discipline, cleanliness, and the good management of one's time and labor are repeated in English to the students.

The graduation ceremony was instructive. Clinton DeWitt, one of the head instructors of the period, described it as

> [A] pageant in the form of a melting pot, where all men descend from a boat scene representing the vessel on which they came over; down the gangway... into a pot fifteen feet in diameter and seven and a half feet high, which represents the Ford English School. Six teachers, three on either side, stir the pot with ten foot ladles representing nine months of teaching in the school. Into the pot

52 nationalities with their foreign clothes and baggage go, and out of the pot after vigorous stirring by the teachers comes one nationality, viz., American.

S.S. Marquis continues with a laconic observation: "Presently the pot began to boil over and out came the men dressed in their best American clothes and waving American flags." After this, the influential members of the community paid tribute to America with enthusiastic speeches. After the ceremony's end, the new graduates played "American" sports for the rest of the day, while the evening was crowned by a banquet offered by Ford in honor of the "educational" success of the teachers.

This scene—and Ford's general policy, insofar as it is an excessively dramatized form of a banal ritual—is representative of the wave of Americanization that then crossed the United States. More than eight hundred firms across all industrial sectors adopted "Americanization plans" in 1919. Between 1880 and 1924, the year in which the valves of the Old World closed up again, twenty-five million immigrants crossed the Atlantic, the majority of whom did so to find jobs as workers. In this way, between 1880 and the middle of the 1920s, progress ends up being intimately connected to the constitution of the "American people." One becomes the condition of the other. At present, progress and people form a combined pair whose contemporary disjunction accompanies the slow decline of the United States. Even if it doesn't signal the dissolution of this combinatory technique, the decline nevertheless underlines the failure of the superposition progress/people. The incredible innovation represented by the Model T assembly line also depended on a new model, not only of workers, but of "people." Technology is far from solely a technical affair—lodged behind a simple tool lies an order of the world.

Fresh out of the mass market, the American demos of the first years of Fordism crystallized in the notion of a *standard of living*. Accessing a "higher living standard" and becoming as white as possible constituted the salient traits of the American people, such as it was invented at the dawn of the twentieth century (and would appear up until the lively eruptions of the next century). Americanization plans taught nothing other than this psychological structure, which was also incorporated in the new technological inventions of America, from the light bulb to the telegraph. In 1929, a working family in Detroit, where access to gas, water, heat, and health care were widespread, consumed fifteen times more than a European family, and its living conditions were incomparably superior to those of a family in Berlin, Frankfurt, or London. Moreover, Ford's employees constantly renewed their mass consumer goods: radios, phonographs, electric irons, vacuum cleaners, etc. Finally, while more than half of American families bought a car, no working family then had the means to acquire one in Europe. For the first time, the United States "objectively" demonstrated a formidable progress in relation to Europe, on whom they could now impose their own criteria and categorizations. In an unprecedented way, the idea that Americanization, the mass market, access to goods, and world peace are consubstantial began to make inroads in Europe. The unity of the "American people" could even turn out to be more solid than that of any European "people," and such bravado couldn't remain without a response from the other side of the ocean.

In 1932, François Simiand published a work entitled *Le Salaire, l'évolution sociale et la monnaie* (*The Salary: Social Evolution and Money*), in which he intended to settle accounts with the notion of the standard of living. According to Simiand, in order to understand what a "higher standard of living" is, one must not only look at buying power (cash), the number of calories ingested, the number of clothes bought, etc., but also displace one's observation toward that which doesn't strictly pertain to the economic sphere: gifts and mutual services, for example—or what one would later call "the sharing economy." Thus, the idea of the "people" produced by America washes ashore in the "old" Europe, which continues to consider the people in terms of vital space and conquest, not world peace and the acceptance of generic being. The old Europe was still dreaming of racial empires and exporting Enlightenment by commerce or by sword. Every European nation remained persuaded of its own historic civilizing mission and competed with others for this title. The United States considered itself superior to the old bourgeois Europe, rigidified in its consumption by moral codes and hierarchical strata. In America, mass consumption produced by ricochet a certain equity in the redistribution of goods, and thus a relatively happy and serene people, unburdened of the apocalyptic visions of the future that maintained it was necessary to either overthrow dominant classes or fight for racial survival.

At least this is how Ford liked to imagine it for himself. He neglected to consider the risk that his techniques and visions of the world might be appropriated ill-advisedly. His first book, *My Life and Work*, which appeared in 1922, was one of Hitler's favorite works—which is not a coincidence. The year 1922 also saw the death of the famous economist Simon Nelson Patten, the author of *The New Basis of Civilization* (1907), in which Patten devised the well-known saying that American capitalism will make the Western world pass from a "civilization of scarcity" to a "civilization of abundance." Man would then know no more "interruptions." If humanity would only turn toward American psychology, this avant-garde of the future psychology of the world consumer, Patten prophesied an unprecedented anthropological turning point that would entail a total disruption of the psychological structure for the humanity of the new century. This thesis was not without sense. While Europeans were haunted by famines until 1950, in the United States an enormous reservoir of resources had permitted Americans to benefit from favorable nutritional intake since 1870.

As German economist Werner Sombart confirms following Tocqueville, what really changes in the United States is not the absence of disparities in revenue. These, in the United States as elsewhere, remain enormous. It is the absence of an entire apparatus of distinctions like those inherited from the Ancien Régime and retained by bourgeois society. As a corollary, class consciousness is replaced by "being American." In the twenties, the idea that each American more or less possessed the "standard of living" of his people achieved consensus. To return to Ford, the very notion of a "high cultural salary" radically broke with the old American—and European—conception of the salary as that which must assure the strict minimum for workers to reproduce their labor force. This change was contemporaneous with new economic and social theories, such as those of Patten or economist Thorstein Veblen, which intended to break with the catastrophist theories of Thomas Robert Malthus still in vogue in the Europe of the twenties. Thus the American people is defined as a community of consumer habits and physical and moral properties linked to access to consumer goods. These are the only criteria one could bring together in a minimal definition of "being American." All this is quite far from the national definitions of what it meant to be an Italian, German, or French person of the same period. This obtundation of the products of the market is so strong that the first serious study on social stratification, carried out in the twenties by Paul Nystrom, conceived social classes in terms of access to goods and no longer in terms of the opposition class/individual. For Nystrom and others, classes were instead characterized according to their "buying power." If a people were now determined by their habits of "American" consumption, a new conception of democracy, according to which "consuming is voting," could come in to being. In this way, social justice and the reduction of disparities mainly spread through access to consumption and thus buying power in the United States. From the experience of the Grangers, a coalition of Midwestern farmers that combated monopolies after the American Civil War, to the populism of the twenties, the language of change, progress, and populism underwent a singularly consumerist turn.

In the words of Victoria de Grazia's *Irresistible Empire*, a true inspiration for this text, on one side of the Atlantic there is an old regime of consumption, and on the other, in America, "a new regime of consumption." The old regime is understood differently with regard to problematics of race, empire, and class, without mentioning its evident wariness of the new. In 1926, the sociologist André Siegfried noted that the American technical jargon that inundated Europe at the time sought to give itself an appearance of neutrality, though it actually embodied "a conception of man, society, and life" absolutely contrary to that of Europe. The reason for this opposition is not that the *American standard of living* was undesirable in itself. It was that, in the Europe of the twenties and thirties, where a multitude of factions competed for resources and hegemony, realizing this standard was simply impossible.

At the time, many were fascinated by Fordism's capacity to respond to economic problems and transform subjectivities, thanks to the new technosocial apparatuses he invented. Hitler, but also Antonio Gramsci, Werner Sombart, or even Friedrich von Gottl-Ottlilienfeld and his "white socialism," saw in Ford an inspirational genius. What they nevertheless rejected was the fact that consumer society dissolved the people as a cultural entity into a generic people defined only by its material habits of consumption. At the end of the thirties and after the New Deal, however, the idea that the solution to the economic crisis depended on consumption made its way to Europe, as the theories of John Maynard Keynes demonstrate. Two opposing solutions, the Popular Front and Nazism, presented themselves. In 1936, in France, Prime Minister André Léon Blum decided to lower the workweek to forty hours while maintaining identical salaries and granting the first paid vacations. The Under Secretary of State for Sport and the Organization of Leisure was created, after the example of the socialist Léo Lagrange. On the other side of the Rhine, Hitler, like a German Ford, promised he would rush the country's late arrival to consumer access and prevent the formation of a Popular Front.

It is to the sociologist Maurice Halbwachs' credit to have clearly understood what was then in the works with the following remark: while market democracy, in its capacity to produce new desires, could break the hierarchy of needs so proper to Europe, the style of life adapted by workers no longer depended on their conditions of work and cultural pressures. In other words, Halbwachs wanted to bring an end to an idea of determinism that prevented taking seriously how consumer society liberated workers from a certain determinism in their living conditions. In *L'évolution des besoins dans les classes ouvrières* (*The Evolution of Needs in the Working Classes*, 1933), he shows how, by way of consumption, workers make aesthetic and social choices that can differentiate them from their neighbors, also workers. Halbwachs reveals the capacity of consumer society—and thus of America—to transform the historical consciousness of workers in such a way that they abandon all political consciousness in favor of an Americanization, which is to say, consumer status. The sociologist argues that the distinction between true and false desires has become anachronistic, because all the cultural gadgets of America, as "technical language," produce a new consciousness that, for its part, is truly embodied in the subjects of market society. In this way, Halbwachs defended the model of rising consumption promoted by the Popular Front *as a means of short-circuiting* the epoch's destiny. In the crosshairs, he saw the risk of a total war of peoples in the name of the hierarchy of needs and their cultural superiority—a war that everyone dreads, not without reason.

After the trial of World War II, in the form of the Marshall Plan, the United States tried to impose this same constitutive mechanism from their history on a Western Europe worn out and ruined by imperial dreams. The idea of the Marshall Plan would be to produce a market of American consumption in Europe, in such a way as to unify it by integrating it in the cultural consensus of a globalized market democracy. The growing destabilization of Europe and its project is thus accompanied by a return of populism today, exactly like the United States. The failure of a unified consumer society, which very few had predicted until quite recently, is the very failure of an *American vision of the world*. Thus, with the current shipwreck of the *Pax Americana* also sinks the possibility of a democratic and social peace that passes through a "European people."

FRAGMENT ON CAMPS

The waves of U.S. populist protest in the wake of the 2008 crisis were the first signs of the riptide tearing through the present order. While the energies of these public gatherings and square occupations in the United States were in part channeled and absorbed into the calmer waters of 2016's electoral process by way of Bernie Sanders and Donald Trump, the question remains as to how, in relation to the *figure of the camp*, the coming movements might experiment with forms of exodus from the logic of populist capture. Some friends have spoken of the riot, the blockade, and the occupation as that which forms "the *basic* political grammar of the epoch," with which we wouldn't disagree. But to speak of the camp is to speak of another temporal declension of struggle. Yet opposing occupation and camp would also obfuscate the precarious becoming-camp of the occupations of squares, which took place on urban terrains otherwise thoroughly governed by the enemy. The persistence of the occupations was in part due to the new relations and uses encampments put into play, experiments whose participants felt were worth defending. In contrast to the *deferral of time* of the false prophets of the assembly, eternally competing over the future in their bureaucratic zeal for proposals and programs, the apostles of the camp took hold of a time that worked away at the difference between ends and means.

The camp might be said to unfold as a confluence time punctuated by a here-and-now time. Confluence, from *confluere*, means to flow together. It is also a technical term used in riverine ecology to designate a site at which canals, rivers, tributaries, or other bodies of water meet. What is it that happens when such bodies meet? Sometimes a tributary is overwhelmed by the forces of a larger river and is subsumed in it. At other times, like at the Encontro das Águas near Manaus, Brazil, two bodies don't commingle but merely run alongside each other. Sometimes when our bodies meet, there is a spiritual flood that creates a situation—which for the police and the state becomes completely unmanageable—that makes it impossible for us to return to the way things were before. It is by the working of a confluent spirit, by way of love and the camp's encounter of different forms of life, that we attempt to come to terms with others with whom we don't share a language, with friends, with the limits of our purity. While their act was understandable at the time, the *will to ideological purity* of the civil rights movement's Student Nonviolent Coordinating Committee caused them to miss an opportunity provided by the camp in 1968. Citing its ostensibly "reformist" character, the Committee abstained from being involved with Resurrection City, a protest camp in Washington, DC, organized by Martin Luther King's Poor People's Campaign. The camp ended in riots and succeeded through its failure, weaving a fabric of unprecedented exchange between Chicanos, Blacks, Indigenous peoples, and poor whites that resulted in new forms of power and organization.

The camp bears witness to the life of a calling. The religious camp meeting, an incarnation of Protestant romantic excess, appeared in Kentucky at the beginning of the nineteenth century. It was an anxious time of capital's ascent, when old forms of cooperativism gave way to new relations of competition. What distinguished the camp meeting from previous revival forms was that the faithful came prepared to camp, a change that "produced an extraordinary religious experience" (Ellen Elsinger). While one cannot deny the violent conditions of the settler-colonial frontier in which the camp meeting appeared, it also reorganized social divisions according to a shared belonging. *Campus*, from which camp derives, indicates a level surface or field, and the camp rearticulated relationships through a kind of leveling operation. In spite of their social status, everyone in the early camps slept in wagons, and later in tents. The presence of Blacks participating in and preaching at the camp meetings signaled a departure from the prior segregated religious forms; in some cases, even children would preach if they were so moved by the spirit. The first camp meeting came about through a series of services in which the fervor of a band of ministers provoked a response from the congregation, a kind of spiritual expectation unfulfilled by the mere administration of the communal sacrament. Gradually the clergy, many of whom were experienced in the art of revivalism, responded through the formulation of an invitation to regeneration near the end of the service, and soon the centrality of the sacrament was displaced by the call to a new life.

As foreign as the camp meeting may be to our experience, something of a spiritual calling is undeniably operative in what resonates and beckons us together, in flight from the despair of our empty time. This was the case in Ferguson, Missouri, when ten young people, who met during the first protests after the police murdered Michael Brown, began camping out together on West Florissant Avenue. They called themselves Lost Voices, then quickly changed their name to Found Voices. In the words of one of their members, the 23-year-old former Crip Dontey Carter, the time of being together and camping in the street was one of "a spiritual awakening":

> I just showed up and people was chanting together. And so I chanted, and started making some different chants . . . and I went to a bigger crowd and the same thing. It was a natural, spiritual thing to me to just keep doing this. . . . My life changed radically. . . I had friends die left and right—drugs, gangs, violence—and I've pulled away from all of that, working for the movement. . . . Once we were lost but now we are found. . . We were the Lost Voices, but then people got a hold of who we really are, what this movement is truly about. We're not lost anymore.

Though Carter was a fervent disciple and leader of the movement who often called for the indictment of the murderous police officers, he frames the movement's appeal in different terms. What drew him away from gang life was the proposition of what was shared in the protest, a new life chanting and camping against the violence of the state. For the Found Voices, the encampment on West Florissant offered a departure from the perilous path of the world, a time in which the lost are found.

In contrast to the experimental camps of the squares, those of Standing Rock made use of a sacred tradition that contains within it the promise of redemption. The Sun Dance is a traditional encampment of the Sioux in which prayers and dancing assure the acquisition of spiritual power and an "abundance of good things" for the people (Michael Melody). During the Indian Wars, the innovations of the Ghost Dance enacted a variation of the practice of the sacred camp exemplified in the Sun Dance and made a particular use of it. The Ghost Dance emerged in the teachings of the Paiute shaman and prophet Wovoka. On the first day of 1889, Wovoka had a vision during the solar eclipse foretelling the defeat of the white man and the return of a peaceful world. The ceremonial ghost dances communicated in Wovoka's vision would hasten the arrival of the Messiah and the forces of dead spirits to give strength to the Indian nations in the coming wars. Shortly after Wovoka received his vision, the Lakota warrior Kicking Bear went to visit him and delivered his teaching to the Sioux people upon his return:

> My brothers, I bring to you the promise of a day in which there will be no white man to lay his hand on the bridle of the Indian's horse. . . . I bring you word from your fathers the ghosts, that they are now marching to join you, led by the Messiah who came once to live on earth with the white men, but was cast out and killed by them. I have seen the wonders of the spirit-land, and have talked with the ghosts. I traveled far and am sent back with a message to tell you to make ready for the coming of the Messiah and return of the ghosts in the spring.

The ceremonial Ghost Dance camp testified to the promise of the redemption of the dead and provided a spiritual form that accompanied Sioux resistance. In 1890, a series of battles known as the Ghost Dance War culminated in the massacre of hundreds of Lakota camped at Wounded Knee Creek. Eighty years later, the gesture of the American Indian Movement's armed occupation of the town of Wounded Knee on the Pine Ridge Indian Reservation in 1973 evoked this memory of the massacre, as did the camps of the water protectors of Standing Rock when they appeared a few hours away from Wounded Knee in 2016. History presents these events in a discontinuous form, though the time of the camp bears within itself the unbroken continuity of a remembrance, a testament to the Sioux's prior way of life. Though the Sun Dance was outlawed for thirty years at the beginning of the twentieth century, it continued clandestinely, then underwent a revival in the second half of the century. The sacred camp of the Sioux is inextricably bound to the life of a place and to the life of the earth. It goes without saying the resolve of an unwavering tradition to defend the earth from capital's penultimate decimations, in our time of geographical and spiritual rootlessness, has the capacity to *move us*. In the wake of Standing Rock, several other camps have appeared. From Two Rivers Camp in west Texas, to the Split Rock Sweetwater Prayer Camp of the Ramapough Lenape in the mountains of northeastern New Jersey, to the L'eau Est La Vie Camp in the bayous of Louisiana, and Camp Makwa, organized by the Anishinaabe in northern Minnesota, the camp is put to use to blockade the passage of the "black snake."

The traditional form of the Sun Dance camp involved several days of a profane camp followed by a sacred camp. At the profane camp, the community would make the necessary preparations for the performance of the rituals that would take place during the sacred camp (Michael Melody). In a similar way, a friend at Standing Rock spoke of the life of the camp as essentially a time of preparation and prayer punctuated by the attacks made on the advance of the black snake. In this sense, the camp is a camp of anticipation, thrust into tension between a time of confluence and a here-and-now time.

Distinct from the rooted camps of tradition, the hobo encampments or "jungles" of the last century provided a communal form for the hobos' fundamentally nomadic life. In this the jungle resembled that prototypically nomadic camp of messianic promise, the camp of the Israelites, organized around the Tabernacle in the wilderness. As the *Book of Numbers* relates, above the Tabernacle hovered a cloud by day and a pillar of fire by night, and whenever "the cloud lifted from the tent, the Israelites struck camp, and at the place where the cloud settled, there they pitched their camp." In a similar fashion, in the suburban wilderness outside of towns and near the intersection of train lines, the portable jungle organized the life of workers and the unemployed (Nels Anderson). The description of A.W. Dragstedt offers an image of the life of a jungle, located half a mile from a railroad intersection on the edge of a strip of forest:

> The new arrivals walk up to the fire, look over the bunch to find, perhaps, some old acquaintances. Then some of us find seats or lie down.... The feed is open to everybody. Bread and sausage are brought out; even sugar is passed around as long as it lasts. The men eat in silence.... Daylight comes.... Fires are started, cooking

> utensils are chosen. The law of the jungle is that no one can call a vessel his except at the time he uses it. Packages and receptacles are opened revealing food of all kinds. Eating commences. If any man with more than enough for himself sees someone else not eating, it is etiquette to offer to share with his neighbor. If the other man accepts the offer, he thereby takes upon himself the responsibility of cleaning the dishes. . . . Talking goes on as long as the daylight lasts. Heated arguments often develop. Papers and pamphlets are distributed, union cards are taken out; business meetings are held to decide policies and actions, how to get the next meal or how to win the battle between labor and capital.

Though the abject conditions that contributed to the law of the jungle's particular communism should not be romanticized, they offered the prospect of a common power that resonates with our time. Their abjection was fueled by the brutality of capital's ascent, ours by that of its decadence. A Wobbly jungle played a pivotal role in fights for free speech rights, which involved a series of struggles fought to secure public spaces for organizing efforts. One day after the organizer Frank Little was arrested in October 1910, a large Wobbly jungle appeared along the railroad tracks south of Fresno, California. In a kind of early swarming tactic, these "undesirable characters" arrived from all over the country to offer support and to crowd the streets of the city to organize on street corners and soapboxes. By the night of Little's arrest, around fifty Wobblies had already arrived from Los Angeles, while more were on their way from Spokane, Portland, and St. Louis, and Little was soon freed. The jungle fulfilled an important role for hobos in their search for work and the capacity to circulate and participate in distant struggles. Like the sacred camp, the jungle war machine was not a "political" form per se, but its practices could be *put to use* in the battles of the workers' movement.

If anything, in the end, the history of the camp testifies to the fact that whatever revolutionary practice need not be relegated—as it is in certain teachings of the gospel of political economy—to the obscure metaphysics of the proletariat's second coming, for which many still wait in vain. At the same time, it is only with great arrogance or great uncertainty one could really say *what should be done*, friends, much less we who have barely avoided losing ourselves to the world. Yet the lesson of the camp indicates it is in the *how* and not the *what* of our doing, in the mode and the manner the calling carries out its work, like the cloud and the pillar of fire. It is a fracture that passes through us, which is to say *our lives*, according to the uses made of what we do and what we have. Let the figure of the camp call us to experiment with forms, attentive to their potentials, that we be caught up in a time that we seize and in which we are seized! Let us not miss the *chance* of the failures to come, where we will sharpen the art of being in and not of the world!

K-POPULISM

The equation of truth-telling with betrayal is one of the more powerful ways to promote silence. No one wants to be regarded as a traitor.

—bell hooks

Let's begin with a conjuration. To put it simply, we must ward off the state of normality we face at every level. Today we see the normality of the liberal democratic order under attack around the globe. At the same time, we must remind ourselves that what seems to threaten it is actually disgustingly tiresome and boring. In some sense, this is an *extreme normality* of capital and the state, complicit with the desperately networked and nationalized desires *of the people*. Here we also face the possible eruption of a war of an entirely different magnitude—but wouldn't that also be extremely normal?

Detesting these popular alt-normalities, we look for ways to analyze and engage. Certainly this is how we meet each other. And we admit that we do not have a definitive answer. Situated in a peninsula, which has repeatedly become the crux of conflicts and struggles in East Asia, we remember that our bodies harbor different memories and histories than those of Europe and the Americas. Different revolutions and counter-revolutions, different forms of colonization and war.

We do not appoint ourselves as some legitimate choice, even in our faintest imagination. Speaking in no proper name, we attempt to communicate and translate our collective conditions, which are by no means in agreement or homogeneous. Some of us live in the metropolis, in spaces scheduled for eviction, demolition, and redevelopment. Others live in the country, farming and working in the fields or protesting unending environmental destruction. Others of us live outside the peninsula. All of us try to write, but aspire to compose a materialist transversality—a wholesale subversion and transformation—rather than some form of cultural critique. We have nothing to gain or lose, so would like to reach out to our friends here, elsewhere and nowhere, to ask whether there is any condition for the expansion of a common within and beyond our limits.

SCENE AFTER SCENE

The spectacular scene rules Korean politics today. From the candlelight scene to the electoral scene of South Korean President Moon Jae-in to the scene of uncannily ubiquitous hipsters, enamored with their selfies, the scenes go on and on. Perhaps this is happening everywhere, but here the intensity of its proliferation leads to our exhaustion, and even when we are somehow captured in the shot, we refuse to pose.

SCENE ONE: THE SCANDAL OF CHOI SOON-SIL

From late October to December of 2016, crowds of South Koreans filled the streets every Saturday in freezing weather. It was arguably the largest popular demonstration the country has ever seen. At its peak, on December 3, Gwanghwamun Square and adjacent roads were packed with over two million people. The main stage was set up and decked out with sound and lighting systems, making it seem more like an arena rock concert than a demonstration. Musicians performed and citizens took turns making speeches onstage, as the sea of thousands of candle-waving people completed the scene. The riot police, who would normally number in the tens of thousands, were mostly forced to the sidelines, unable to challenge the people. In a country where police are ready to unleash an abundant force, how had this come to be?

What triggered the event was the revelation of Choi Soon-sil's secret machinations, then personal confidant of former president Park Geun-hye. The damning trails of Soon-sil's transactions had slowly emerged fact by fact since the summer of 2016. It was first reported Soon-sil had made covert deals with major corporations, like Samsung and LG. Another report saw her pressuring university teachers to give preferential treatment to her daughter, who was admitted to a prestigious women's university as an "Olympic-prospect" equestrian. This generally enraged teenagers oppressed by the hellish examination system, but in particular the students and graduates of the university who came out as a mass to protest in the streets. Gathering together in a bloc, they refused to participate in the classical social movement. Another leak was the damning evidence of her intervention in Geun-hye's presidential speechwriting. A photograph of Soon-sil, with her right hand on a tablet PC, turning obliquely and frowning toward the viewer, spread everywhere. And it was this image of Big Sister Choi covertly pulling strings that provided fuel for the public's rage and gave the popular upheaval a distinct hue. As the scandal officially developed into "Choi Soon-sil-Gate," the populace turned on Park. The refrain "Park Geun-hye, Down and Out!" (박근혜 하야) spread and became an informal call in the streets.

SCENE TWO: SHIPWRECK WITH SPECTATORS

The infamous sinking of the ferryboat *MV Sewol* off the southwestern coast on April 16, 2014, was a major shock to South Koreans. The incident took 304 lives, many of whom were high school students on a school trip.

As an outraged nation absorbed a flood of information, what became apparent was the authorities' total incompetence and disregard for the victims' suffering. Many witness accounts proliferated, telling of how the rescue workers did nothing and bided their time while the capsized ship slowly reached the ocean floor. Some waited for orders. Others kept referring to the boundaries of jurisdiction or the chain of command. "Is this even a nation?," muttered the devastated people, initiating a refrain whose repetition would eventually drive Park Geun-hye from power.

The major news sources headed by friends of Park Geun-hye circulated a range of stories that spoke of heroic rescue efforts and visits by benevolent, grave-faced dignitaries. Independent media provided counterpoints and other perspectives, and rumors, speculations, and conspiracy theories abounded. In appearance, truth was everywhere, while sensible truths remained unseen.

The collective experience of the *Sewol* had a certain lived quality, a *duration*, which became infused with South Korean everyday life. Emanating from submerged spaces, texts, voicemails, and photos the teenagers had sent to loved ones from their phones were shared in everyday gestures through the screen. For many, the experience of repeated shocks brought through a cell phone surpassed the threshold of the very appearance of normality.

This everyday absurdity dislocated the normal banality of life, rendering it dysfunctional and revolutionary.

Afterward, demonstrations ensued. At almost every step the victims' families and their supporters took toward the president, they were faced with the police. Hundreds of miles from the presidential palace, the riot police blocked the protesters' march, like bees protecting their hive and its queen. At first, they were cautious, but their determination eventually turned into a violence of absurd proportions. This was then perversely mimicked by the forces of the Far Right, through harassment, insults, and raw violence. It was a sad parody of the "get a job or buy a house" normality enacted by the fascists. South Koreans bore witness to an unprecedented and absurd violence, all in the name of Park Geun-hye.

THE PARK DYNASTY AND THE REPUBLIC

The power and machinations of Park Geun-hye were deeply rooted in the foundation of modern Korean history, further fracturing the southern half of a peninsula already fractured by the Korean War. The autocratic rule of Park Geun-hye's father, Park Chung-hee—who took power with a military coup in 1961 coincided with an intense anti-communism as well as the nation's rapid industrialization.

Today a segment of the population still admires, if not worships him. Those over sixty, whose horizon of collective memory extends back to the Korean War, or even Japanese colonial rule, attest to how things have improved. They look at the past with satisfaction and pride, now living in an industrialized society where, even though they might struggle to make ends meet, people no longer starve.

Park Chung-hee was assassinated in 1979, five years after his wife had succumbed in an earlier attempt on his life. Having lost both parents, then twenty-something Geun-hye became the tragic orphan princess of the agrarian society's dead king and queen, sacrificed on the altar of the Korean industrial revolution. Park Geun-hye, elected president in 2013, completed the appearance of a cycle initiated by the rise and fall of her father and the miracle of the modern industrial nation. While her father was the martyred king, Park Geun-hye—once the nation's innocent and valiant maiden princess—was elected President Queen.

While one segment of the republic admires them, another segment deeply mistrusts the Park dynasty and its minions. For them, the notion they are the nation's benevolent saviors is nothing less than pure absurdity. Born primarily after 1960, they have either participated in the eighties' democratization movement or at least inherited its legacy. This movement involved the urban poor, factory workers, and radicalized students who formed an alliance in a general strike and street confrontations against the rule of the military junta of Chun Doo-hwan, who took power in 1980 following Park Chung-hee's assassination. Chun was responsible for the massacre of the Gwangju Uprising that same year. The simmering social upheaval saw its peak in 1987, when Chun had no choice but to promise to step down and institutionalize the national presidential ballot. With his departure, the South Korean liberal democratic order was born.

For decades, these two segments have set the stage for Korean politics. Although such a segmentation has congealed in domestic politics, its dimensions are conditioned, contained, and affected by the North-South segmentation and the Cold War. The spectacular politics of the scene is a later development. Today the scenes permeate the segments and, while the latter are still active, they seem to be in a transitory stage.

SCENE THREE: GANGNAM STATION MURDER

On May 17, 2016, a woman in her twenties was brutally murdered by a 34-year-old man in a unisex bathroom near Gangnam Station, located in the middle of the affluent district referenced in the eponymous hit "Gangnam Style." When asked about his motive, the murderer said, "I did it because women have always ignored me my entire adult life."

As the news reverberated across social media, Exit 10 of Gangnam Station was covered with post-it messages, expressing sadness and anger in solidarity with a common plight. The post-it notes, whose marketed function is to offer a convenient, disposable means of creating reminders for to-do tasks, were transformed into embattled, minimalistic *Daejabo*[1] or *Dazibao* (대자보, 大字報) for the cellular networked society. In short, it was a call

1. First introduced in Beijing by a university student in 1957 to express doubts about a student election's procedure, *Daejabo* refers to a wall-mounted newspaper or similar item often used as a form of protest.

to action, a machine of contagion temporarily transforming the everyday personal and political.

Misogyny was thus identified and exposed as a social problem. Feminism, hitherto largely limited to the elite realm of the academy and activist circles, became popular. Reading groups sprang up everywhere and women came out and marched on the streets of Gangnam and beyond.

CONVERGENT SCENES: THE 2017 CANDLELIGHT REVOLUTION

The composition and frames of the above-mentioned scenes eventually converged and collided in what has been called the Candlelight Revolution. This convergence led to the realization of the candlelight scene, which eventually succeeded in ousting Park Geun-hye and electing Moon Jae-in to the presidency.

While the orderly populace that attended the occupation of Gwanghwamun Square every Saturday certainly inherited the classical twentieth century mold that pitted the democratic segment against the right-wing Park royalists, the convergence of indignation over the *Sewol* disaster and the Choi Soon-sil scandal significantly expanded a populist base. Although the issues surrounding *Sewol* and Choi were quite different in regard to both their origin and content, they shared the common desire to restore to the nation a proper form of government.

The feminist impetus, on the other hand, made its presence felt by confronting the candlelight movement's latent misogyny. In fact, populist attacks on Park Geun-hye had often lowered themselves to criticize her femininity ever since her inauguration, a trend that continued well into the candlelight scene. The three women—Park Geun-hye, Choi Soon-sil, and her daughter—became prime targets in speeches, songs, signs, and visual art. However, the presence of a feminism beyond discourse as a contingent in the demonstration brought pressure to bear on the whole scene, rendering inoperative previously unquestioned expressions of misogyny.

HEGEMONY OF SCENES

Over the last decade, the scene in Korea has become hegemonic in relation to a certain territoriality of struggles, and the Candlelight Revolution was a culmination of this trend. In this sense, contrasting the candlelight demonstration of 2008 to the subsequent mass protests in the second decade of this century can be illustrative. The protest against the trade agreement to import U.S. beef quickly expanded to encompass various other issues of neoliberal society. For two months, protesters gathered daily in Gwanghwamun Square to demand the resignation of Lee Myung-bak. At first numbering in the hundreds, the protesters rapidly grew, and the Square reached seven hundred thousand at its peak.

Incidentally, the Korean social movement of the 2000s, and especially its leftist contingent, did not exist in isolation, but was very much a part of the wave of global justice movements of the late 1990s and early 2000s. It shared the scenes and terrains of the antiglobalization movement through its participation in struggles against the institutions of global capitalism (GATT, WTO, APEC, etc.).

The protestors of 2008 did not shy away from confronting the police. They broke through heavily fortified containment walls made up of cargo containers and riot police vehicles on more than a few occasions. At one time, the protestors seriously asked themselves, after out-maneuvering the enemy, whether storming the presidential palace was an option. They decided not to, unable to imagine what they would do afterward.

The candlelight demonstration of 2008 was also arguably the first square protest that made tactical use of the Internet. A significant number of self-organized individuals and groups systematically used cell phones and laptop computers to exchange real-time information on the ground. In the world prior to smartphones and social media, individual and group volunteers became "one-person media" and provided DIY livestreaming on the Internet. Information from Google Earth and online traffic cameras were also used for countersurveillance, in order to identify the maneuvers of the police.

What we need to make clear in relation to their distance from scene production is that most of these actions remained clandestine. Images were a means rather than an end, and in this sense opacity and anonymity were just as valuable as the spectacle. This was, incidentally, a countermeasure against the right-wing media's then vigorous attack on the movement through the circulation of the trope of the "violent protester." When protesters engaged in tactical demolitions, for example, a whole block of protesters would shout at photographers and videographers not to capture the scene. Certain gestures were not a spectacle to be shared, nor a scene to upload and circulate to garner "likes" on the Internet.

This effort toward an autonomous control of the terrain gave way, however, perhaps as in other parts of the world, to absorption into the cellular arrangement of handheld screens and social media in the 2010s. Where people once produced terrains and cartographies to traverse, South Korean protest gave way to the hegemony of the scene.

The point is neither to extol one popular protest over another, nor to indulge in activist nostalgia, but simply to point out the change in the dynamics of terrains and scenes, which have tended toward the latter's domination.

In any case, the movement of 2008 was utterly defeated, disintegrating under the counterattack of a recomposed police and the accumulated fatigue of two months of daily actions, and leaving an enormous sense of apathy in its wake. Even without this fact, the limitations of the candlelight protest were latently present.

Most glaringly from our perspective, the horizon of the movement was inseparably bound up with concerns over national sovereignty. Questions that went beyond the national politics of parties and presidents were excluded, solidifying the generalized order of the enlightened ones—this male-dominated pundit class of center-left-liberal collusion. Democracy today is inseparable from the hegemonic composition of scenes, typified by the now joyous, now teary-eyed face of Moon Jae-in. Indeed, some very talented and devoted artists and activists made a significant contribution to the successful management of the candlelight scene. We can say today—definitively in hindsight—that a hegemony of the scene was a prefigurative politics of the current regime, fully compatible with the normalcy of state and capital.

SCENES AND TERRAINS IN OUR STRUGGLES

Having critically described the recent hegemonic formation of the South Korean scene, we would like to briefly relate how we perceive scenes and terrains as concepts and how they intersect in the movement today.

Obviously, making a scene into some anathema or taboo not to be associated with is not our intention. In fact, such a quasi-religious moralism and posturing is itself a tendency of the kind of scene production we vigorously want to avoid. We have participated in and engaged with various scenes to different degrees, including those we describe above. Needless to say, we may or may not have some prior knowledge about certain scenes. In any case, we cannot know when a certain scene leads onto some other scene or terrain, and vice versa, unless we make some contacts and connections, engage in some form of experimentation.

Perhaps it is already clear that what we mean by a scene here includes the sense evoked by the notion of a spectacle, but it is not limited to it. On the one hand, there is the visual aspect of appearance—its fetishism and commodification. On the other, there is also some communal aspect, as the meaning indicated by an ordinary sense of the word—a place where things happen.

This latter dimension of a scene is obviously more important to us. A scene, in this communal dimension, is constituted by a multiplicity of things, of people, and of other beings. Without scenes, there is no practice. While a scene in this sense is more like a bounded entity with its own ecology, it may become more or less open to the outside, depending on the positions and dispositions of things, people, and beings.

A terrain, on the other hand, indicates a sense of the outside, of an openness, like that of a field. The word itself evokes the physical dimensions of the earth, to be studied and traversed. To have a grasp of a terrain is to not only understand its elements, but also to overcome adversity or adversaries. In our context, a terrain may be a setting, like that of the everyday activities involved with relating to humans and other beings on the land. It might also be a setting in which struggles against the forces of capital and the state occur. This can be grasped concretely as the physical setting of a demonstration, or abstractly as a social field in which political struggles take place. Instead of shying away, eschewing, or glorifying them, we seek a heterogeneous communization of our terrains.

ELLIPSES

Since the end of the Korean War, the South Korean social movement against the forces of capital and the state has relied on the maintenance of a façade of unity and its associated centrality and hierarchy. Various socialized and organized forces of the oppositional segment have maintained the appearance of unity in spite of underlying multiplicities. In the eighties and nineties, unity was centered on the figure of the people (*minjung*). On the one hand, this overlapped with the left-labor politics of the proletariat (*nodongja*), and the left-nationalist politics of the nation (*minjok*) on the other. What is important to note is that the wave of segmentation against the homogenizing forces of the state and capital has consisted of multiplicities, a plane of consistency extending beyond such major focal points of *minjung* or *minjok*, even while the *appearance* of the movement's unity was stressed as a sign of strength.

If the multiplication of specific terrains of struggle and the rupture of a politics of the scene are the result of this contemporary fragmentation, it seems necessary to think of a new geography of struggle in order to better understand our positions and dispositions at the heart of an antagonistic, fragmented field. In this way, we might multiply lines of engagement and embark on new lines of flight.

Between scenes and terrains, we need a map, perhaps imaginary or totally speculative—a mental cartography of our counter-behaviors.

We propose an image-form: that of multiple ellipses instead of perfect concentric circles. If the ellipse seems pertinent to us, it is because, in geometry, the ellipse takes form between two focal points, literally in-between. The simplest definition of an ellipse is a curve drawn on a plane with two focal points in such a way that the sum of the distances between the curve and the two points becomes constant. In addition, an ellipse is a generalized form of a circle, collapsing two focal points on to one location. For example, the earth roughly travels an ellipse whose focal point is the sun.

Ellipses are always-already in the struggle. If one looks at localized struggles in Korea, ellipses are everywhere. The warfare surrounding localized struggles, almost without exception, is waged by a combination of locals or "concerned parties" and activists in residence. Together they resist and travel to the metropolis or to another struggle in order to build a network of solidarity.

If we reduce the complexities *in situ* to a simplistic model, their positionalities mark two elliptical focal points. Thus we conceptualize the nomadic lines the activists and locals draw on the terrain as ellipses of various shapes and proportions.

Another way to derive an ellipse geometrically is through the intersection of a cone. Would not the plane of struggle cut across the cone of our psychic life between pure memory and the sensory motor present—the memory cone proposed by French philosopher Henri Bergson? Does the resulting plane in elliptical form become a field where we share a common suffering and a common joy? We must admit this conceptualization does not quite fit the designated usage of Bergson's original diagram. Moreover, more importantly for us, the cone, plane, and ellipse resulting from this bricolage would not represent the memory of a person, but of a collectivity. This forms a diagram, indicating a different notion of intersectionality we may create between a terrain (plane) and scene (memory).

What we want to bring to light is the existence of another approach to the paths running between scenes and terrains. To identify with local intensities is to form around them a protective circle. Distancing oneself from them is betrayal. With such a hypothesis of the ellipse, we not only want to describe a certain collapse of the revolutionary movement and a dispersion of its forces, but open a planetary discussion as to how we might conceive of new territorializations of struggle. Neoliberalism, after all, acts on a global scale by the production of specific terrains.

THE PEOPLE OF APOCA-LYPSE

Vox Populi, Vox Dei, Salvate

"When the pagans spoke about the world, what interested them was always its beginnings, and its leaps from one cycle to another, but now there is nothing but an End lying at the limit of a long flat line. Necrophiliacs, we are no longer interested in anything but this end, since it is definitive... The Apocalypse is not a concentration camp (Anti-christ); it is the great military, police, and civil security of the new State (the Heavenly Jerusalem). The modernity of the Apocalypse lies not in its predicted catastrophes, but in its programmed self-glorification, the institution of glory in the New Jerusalem, the demented installation of an ultimate judiciary and moral power."

—Gilles Deleuze, *Essays Critical and Clinical*

"Either to accept, henceforth, this end for what it will be when it will have taken place: a simple fact about which there is nothing to say, except that it is insignificance itself—something that deserves neither exaltation nor despair nor even attention. Or else to work to elevate the fact to concept and empty negation to negativity."

—Maurice Blanchot, *Friendship*

LANDSCAPE 1: ENDS WITHOUT END—SEASONS COME UNDONE, MELODIES ARE LOST, AND NEVERTHELESS NOTHING CHANGES

The world crumbles under our feet. As the fiction of progress fades, the apocalyptic affect smacks our little heads. There is nothing new in a century that struggles to truly begin, only our humors are now marked by *acute dysphoria*.

Now our planet, once imagined eternally puncturable at will, recoils. From a geophysical and biological point of view, the Earth suffers. At multiple shared points across the globe, this presents itself as a gigantic, diffuse crisis of human worlds. The epoch of the absence of a future had already invaded the time of the twentieth century, if not some time before. This doesn't matter. Each epoch has always had its Nostradamuses. Only today we do nothing but await the arrival of zombies, or viruses, or tears of suffering and pain. The press tells us the sixth mass extinction has just started and nevertheless *nothing changes*. We are the incessant witnesses of both the huge and small continuous catastrophe. Although we *already* live the end of epochality, as both a physical and metaphysical closure, in our camp a difficult observation emerges. If even we who take part in the disaster feel the unavoidable need to act, to find by any means some firm grasp on the world, our forms of political organization offer exceedingly obsolete responses to the urgency of the situation. Our common abandonment of the world is written in fictions that evermore distance *us* from our own becoming. Our present, even in the medium term, becomes unimaginable outside the cognitive frame of catastrophe, dystopian science fiction and messianic eschatology.

If we had to characterize our affliction we would say that, at the individual level, it appears with the very possibility of the end of the world and the explosion of a gigantic crisis of presence. *We are caught up in an impresence of the impresent.*

The anthropologist Ernesto de Martino dedicated the largest part of his life to studying the forms of the crisis of presence, the end of the world of magic and its disenchantment. Unfortunately, he died before completing a final study on modernity's apocalyptic character. In the sketch of a project of systematic study, however, he was able to grasp the extreme novelty of this "disposition proper to our epoch" that is a "permanent abandonment to the lived experience of the end." According to this formulation, a dissolution into the end now happens without eschaton or ultimate finality. Today the twilight of modernity is reduced to an eternal catastrophe, to a never-ending end.

The theme of the end is present in Western culture outside all religious horizons of salvation, as a desperate catastrophe of the worldly, the domestic, the familiar, the sensible and the useful. It is a catastrophe that relates with meticulous, even obsessional, care the disintegration of the ordered world, the alteration of the domestic, the loss of the familiar, and the practical unavailability of the world.

Our apocalypse without *eschaton* joins what some have seen in these last years as the end of the Holocene, or the appearance of the Anthropocene. Today we find ourselves within a new paradox, constructed by a metaphysical problem formulated under the "rigorous" terms of science, of the possibility of humans' terrestrial annihilation. The transformation of humans into an *earth-shattering force*, in other words an "objective" phenomenon, is paid for in turn by the metamorphosis of physics into a subject. The Earth of the scientists again becomes the pagans' Gaia.

It is as if the world took the frightening form of a metastasized body in suffering. The separation of what we once called culture and nature, this ruling myth of modernity, now fades away in the face of an intrusion caused by the opening of the Anthropocene. The surrounded becomes the surroundings. Even if our situation is one of a world crisis in which doctors themselves (but also scientists, philosophers, politicians, and revolutionaries) are *ill*, even if it consists of the most substantial changes in the history of the human, we have not yet drawn the necessary conclusions. A crucial, cruel, and difficult displacement has recently begun doubling its effects in "politics."

Although politics has almost always been configured as a regime of promise and salvation, the political crisis has in reality become a soteriological crisis of finality itself. At the heart of the revolutionary promise, from idealism to materialism, one always found this question of the "reform of consciousness" advocated by the young Marx. This consisted in "making the world aware of its own consciousness, in arousing it from its dream of itself, in explaining its own actions to it," and only ever offered the waking nightmare of being eternally conscious of one's own alienation. Our horizon of expectations no longer means anything but real hallucinations and hallucinatory realities—*endless apocalypse*. One of the most prominent traits of the endless apocalypse is precisely the incredible lucidity with which everyone competes to explain their own acts to the world. *Everyone now has the permanent experience of losing the world and being lost in it.*

In the eighties, while the neoliberal world offensive launched its great attacks against the welfare state and Margaret Thatcher proclaimed that "there is no such thing as society," deconstruction was carrying out its philosophy of suspicion through a contemplation of metanarratives: the end of politics, the end of metaphysics, the end of history, and *the end of the world*. With the liquidation of politics and the great promises of salvation, the nineteenth century "reform of consciousness" was perfected in the form of a self-critical postmodern metaphysics. This anti-metaphysics of deconstruction isn't enough. The intrinsically apocalyptic character of our experience in the world is reduced to the following mutilation: in our daily experience, we have the irreal sense of being in a suspended world, a world that should no longer exist while it has already started to cease existing.

We live an apocalypse without termination or regeneration, one that persists without cessation. For all that, our renunciation of politics is not a renunciation of the world, nor a refusal of its excesses and joys. Our renunciation *reconciles* with the world, in fact, because a world is composed of finitudes.

"Together with the perennial question *when* come whispered lamentations: how much longer will the night of this world last? The end is not just a longing; it is known to be imminent," Jacob Taubes said. In our camp, where every possibility of collective as well as individual redemption has been undermined by skepticism, who could still trust in the future to come, in a finality and its truths? The perspective of Menocchio, a sixteenth-century Friulian miller burned by the Church, who maintained at the stake that "God sees all, but not all the details of what is supposed to happen," offers the overview of a world in which divine ends, chaos, and contingencies don't necessarily enter into contradiction. The end—death—once resembled a beginning under the form of deliverance, a salvation. According to the words of the sixteenth-century mystic, Teresa of Ávila:

> I live without living in myself
> And in such a way, I hope,
> I die because I do not die.

Dying of not dying was the cry of a consciousness close to a higher end, the end of ends, the return of God in his paradise. Misery was not the absence of the end, but the terrible consciousness that one had to patiently await it in virtue of a higher reality, a deliverance. Yet signs are never wrong, and our renunciation of politics comes from the impossibility of the human cry. The lamentation, for decades the preferred litany of the radical Left, signs the latter's incapacity to understand its defeats. One could ask whether they are going to finally grasp the novelty of the situation. In classical politics there is no more salvation, in the social, in strikes, in revolution. They have killed the messiah/revolutionary subject. From now on, the tomorrows that sing have a broken voice. The last survivors of Leninism still await the Great Night as Christians await the Parousia of Christ. The signs of the end cede to the end of all signs. We, who once had the habit of foreseeing the hope of revolutions under the wrinkled skirts of eschatology, find ourselves disoriented in a night without light or limit.

The long path of the West produces a cosmogonic, oceanic movement, a cycle. For us, "in this moment, as a sea recedes, life withdraws." Our unhappiness—feeling the sun weather our lips, weather our hands and our feet, observing the sun's unbearable becoming and the metropoles, full of misery and money, sink away into the twilight of the policed night—our unhappiness is that life retreats endlessly. How could we imagine a destiny in this unhappiness? Losing the world, or losing oneself in it, does not define the limits of the night. On the contrary, it offers an outline of our present, from which we must start in order to explore the latter's limits. "Dying and exceeding one's limits are one and the same," Georges Bataille said.

LANDSCAPE II: TIKKUN

We must no longer organize ourselves based on a revolutionary eschaton, but according to that which resists, conserves, and restores. We have no need of an umpteenth end, but an actual beginning.

From the infernal metropolitan ecologies characterized by industrial dynamics of endless and systematic destruction of all milieus—ecologies whose repercussions are now felt at all stages of the cosmological process and in everything that configures our worlds—have emerged some fragments that still retain some sparks of light.

Le-taken in Hebrew means "repair." From this root, the messianic expression *tikkun ha-olam* was formed. It is a term that designates the *active* process of the reparation of the world. This is a necessary prerequisite to messianic redemption, in which "the just prepare the earth to be the residence of the divine." The question of happiness, salvation, and habitable worlds means nothing other than researching the means to redeem that which can still be redeemed and *repair* that which is to be destroyed. Though the waters of religion recede, leaving behind nothing but swamps and ponds as far as the eye can see, we can still learn from the hope of our elders.

Living organisms, in every sense, are not mechanical assemblages of matter. They have lives and trajectories that are their own. In this sense, they are autonomous. We should start from this conception of the living as an anecdote to the disillusioned, vain, and empty character of our epoch. To announce the following: from the stars to disaster, from protectors of water to those of the earth, that which configures worlds and finitudes within our reach holds a *terrible desire* to save what remains. This consists of a prediction: consider the old machines of the revolutionary movement that intended to work away on a class, modify conditions, educate new souls, speak to the masses, transform society—all this erodes in the face of a huge desire for conservation that attempts by all means to stop the descent of the sea. Each of us perceives the apocalypse without end is the twilight of our life. Our cry there is mute. Disgust with false promises—the death of politics—pushes us toward the banks of irreconcilability and the refusal of all projects, programs, and propositions.

LANDSCAPE III: THE PEOPLE

"Who was it that pressed around Christ to be taught by his words? The people.
Who was it that followed him into the mountains and the desert places to hear his precepts? The people.
Who desired to make him a king? The people.
Who spread their garments and cast branches before him, crying, Hosanna, as he entered Jerusalem? The people."
—Félicité Robert de Lamennais, *Words of a Believer*, 1834

"The goal of civilization: that mankind be people and that people be mankind."
—Victor Hugo, 1860

We will first note that the People is at once myth, mytheme, and historical figure outside of history. Myth and society, myth and community, myth and human life are so inseparable that to say that an idea, thing, or feeling is mythical doesn't provide a sufficient foundation for critique. Myths found partitions of the sensible, experiences, and forms of presences in the world that in turn draw from the myth their force of creation. We ourselves are mythic. Myth is in us and we are contained in it. A myth isn't satisfied with just being a story of the origins of the world. It plunges its roots in the past but speaks to us in the present tense. Myth is this continuous presence, a heady melody whistled by each one of us. Myth doubles and accompanies historical time as much as the lived time of individuals. According to Bronislaw Malinowski, mythical stories "never explain in any sense of the word; they always state a precedent which constitutes an ideal and a warrant for its continuance." The People is this well-known melody that resonates from the depths of the ages. This explains the endless search through time to find the original populist: back to the Romans, the Greeks, or even the Hebrews of Moses. In every epoch, the people precedes the ideal.

In the course of the present disaster, apocalyptic affects do so well at renouncing their ends that History finds itself divided: between events on one side and perpetual apocalypse on the other. We are all now witnesses, prisoners now of our own lucidity. It is here the messianic figure of the People intervenes. After the confusion of every political tradition, the People has never stopped being a repository that begins and realizes modernity's endless apocalypse. Until today, the task of the revolutionary resembled that of the meteorologist looking for the signs of an insurrection in the stormy weather of the people, then working for insurrection according to the signs' interpretation. The task of the reactionary, conservative, or counter-revolutionary consisted in the promise of a restoration, even by forcing the *kathekon* and holding back the very coming of the people. The populist question was thus the *modern* question of politics. For the thinkers of the nineteenth and twentieth centuries, the ruling paradigm dictated either the dissolution of society *in* the people or the dissolution of the people in society. In every case, the model of dissolution was omnipresent, and the concept of the people always carried with it a certain repository of apocalypse. Let's listen to the words of George Sand, taken from the *Letters to the People* of March 1848:

> "It's too soon, we weren't ready; we don't know what to do." No, no—when the popular alarm rattles the vault of the heavens, when the clouds open up, when the veil of the temple tears from bottom to top—it is that the hour is come and the spirit of God will make itself heard. We could have lived ten, twenty, one hundred years in this state of false peace, which was only a monstrous war between the heart and the understanding, without taking one more step toward the truth. Calm and death produce nothing, as you know well, o reasonable and sensible people of France, whose alleged masters increasingly misled in their miserable systems of political economy and government!

The salvation of the People was to always come, but not everyone agreed. The question of knowing whether the people, in the context of their revelation, are Messiah or Catastrophe was one of the central questions that emerged in the wake of the French Revolution.

The People, and with it, the problematic of sovereignty—came to light at the same time "society" extracted itself from the entrails of the Ancien Régime. It consisted of knowing what founds sovereignty—is it the society or the people? Which precedes which? The historical individual, constructed by society, or the political individual, founded with natural rights? This line of questioning opposed, among others, Louis de Bonald and Joseph de Maistre, counter-revolutionaries, to Pierre Leroux and Benjamin Constant, progressives. The essential thing is not the result as much as the terms which defined this infinite debate between counter-revolutionaries and *modern* progressives, a debate which hinged upon the place of the People: "In the traditional society that precedes it and from which it is a tributary," exclaim the conservatives. "In politics, where it is constructed as a sovereign subject," respond the liberals. Yet this question also posed that of liberty. Are the people free and sovereign (the political option), or are they dependent upon and determined by an order and set of traditions from which they cannot wrest themselves without destroying this same order (the social option)?

Pierre Leroux, the inventor of the term socialism in 1834, outlined it in this way: "Our soul is the prey of these two equal and in appearance contrary powers. Our perplexity will only cease when social science has harmonized these two principles (individualism and socialism)." There is not, then, a people *in* society. The people sets itself inevitably *against* society, the people asserts itself *in its heart* as sovereign *against its order.* A society in perfect balance with its people cannot exist, if it is not outside of history, which is to say, outside of politics. The people are precisely a myth trying to fulfill itself. Such was the drama of the first part of the twentieth century, marked by two world wars and the total mobilization of the people, whose figure was subsumed in the body of the nation. It is against this multi-secular myth, against this apocalypse of modernity and its populist excess, that post-World War II politics were slowly constructed. As we will see, this was first and foremost the work of neoliberalism and its slow hegemonic rise. Decades later, the millennium supposedly came to an end, according to the myth of the end of history, accompanied by a belief in good world governance. This project was a crushing failure, as the forceful comeback of the populists teaches us today. The conscience of an apocalypse without end hasn't eroded as much as inaugurated a return to the People, the guarantor of all finality in a society that has abandoned religious for political salvation. The more the old machine of eschatological politics dies, the more the people, this cadaver rejected by the sea, resurfaces. A people who truly, according to Jules Michelet, were "the sea of the future." Was there ever a eulogy written for this people? Who, in our democracies, has sounded the death knell of the people, and when?

In *On Populist Reason*, Ernesto Laclau proposes the invocation of the People as the very condition of democratic action, an operation of these "millions of points in friction that affirm their unity" (D.H. Lawrence). Without the People, frictions dissolve the unity. Anarchy establishes itself as the death of politics. According to Laclau, populism is more a *political logic* than a type of political movement. In truth, this logic is *consubstantial* with politics. Populism is *ontological* to politics as collective action. "The people" is an empty signifier, but not one devoid of signification, because the imprecision and emptiness of the signifier "people" can be signified. The problem is knowing whether this imprecision is the knot of politics or its residue. According to Laclau, utterances such as "society," "nation," or even "politics" are unlimited notions that endlessly increase and can only be enclosed by another concept that erects fields and barriers and seals off and circumscribes the unlimited. This is the function of the signifier "people." Political action, furthermore, must then start from an enclosed determination to act. This is the role of the people—it represents nothing but a certain hegemony. It represents a particular element of "society" that attempts to enclose the very concept of "society" by way of its own hegemonization. The subject that encloses the idea of society is that which makes demands of it as guarantor and repository. This is the first principle of populism.

Moreover, Laclau situates the expression of populism in a specific *rhetorical construction*. At the heart of this construction resides an operation that exceeds the simple art of language. In stylistics, catachresis designates the fact of not being able to literally name a thing, but always having recourse to a figurative sense, for example, "the leg of a chair" or "the teeth of a saw." A lack of language forces a recourse to the figurative.

It is this same lack that haunts the people. *The people* is always a catachresis, a figurative sense that names the literal impossibility of politics. The "people" is the zero point of signification, but also at once, for acting and meaning, its point of departure. This is why a technocrat like Emmanuel Macron is also a populist. The contemporary condition of classical politics cannot surpass the people as a unity of political praxis. In his discourse to the Congress on July 3, 2017, Macron notes:

> We have, you and me, received the mandate of the people. Whether it is given to us by the entire nation or by the voters of a certain constituency changes nothing in its force. Whether it has been supported by direct or indirect suffrage changes nothing in its nature. Whether it has been obtained for some time or very recently at the end of a campaign in which every opinion was ably expressed in its diversity, and whether all of you embody these different opinions, changes nothing about the collective obligation that weighs upon us.

From Laclau, then, we maintain that the People is a prerequisite of classical politics. It becomes the repository as well as first and formal unity of the regime of political promise. It remains to examine the progressive installation of neoliberalism *against* the people, as well as the neoliberal failure to make the people economy. This is how populism and neoliberal discourses have been able to coexist at the heart of neoliberal democracies. In fact, in these last few years, in the style of a heliotropism, the sun of the people dresses up in seductive garments again. It is not lost on whoever compares today with the period from 1890 to 1945 that the people seduced even the most sincere of progressives.

LANDSCAPE IV: NEOLIBERALISM

Walter Lippman's warning was among those that arose against the great populist current of the inter-war period. In 1937, Lippman's work *The Good Society* appears, addressing fascist, Communist, Nazi, and democratic-progressive governmentalities. Each leads to ruin once it succumbs to the idea that it is necessary to plan life in order to govern. At the time, economic, political, and social planning seemed the only way to prop up the head of a capitalist chaos, and the neoliberal cry was heard for the first time:

> Although the partisans who are now fighting for the mastery of the modern world wear shirts of different colors, their weapons are drawn from the same armory, their doctrines are variations of the same theme, and they go forth to battle singing the same tune with slightly different words. Their weapons are the coercive direction of the life and labor of mankind. Their doctrine is that disorder and misery can be overcome only by more and more compulsory organization. Their promise is that through the power of the state men can be made happy.
>
> Throughout the world, in the name of progress, men who call themselves communists, socialists, fascists, nationalists, progressives, and even liberals, are unanimous in holding that government with its instruments of coercion must, by commanding the people how they shall live, direct the course of civilization and fix the shape of things to come.

This book, which resonated in both North America and Europe, brought together a political proposition (the "agenda of liberalism") and a radical critique of collectivism and the old liberalism. In 1938, it is on these precise points that liberal thinkers and heads like Louis Rougier, Raymond Aron, and Louis Marlio came together to assemble a sort of liberal "international" to organize themselves in the face of the imminent catastrophe. More than one hundred intellectuals (economists, journalists, and publicists) from the two continents met in Paris under the auspices of the "Walter Lippmann Colloquium." They all shared a desire to put economic liberty back at the center of human affairs even though, from the New Deal to the USSR, liberalism had been declared clinically dead.

This colloquium inaugurated the constitution of the "liberal current," the only antipopulist option of the 1930s. It also produced a theory of democracy in which the sovereignty of the people comes well after individual rights and market operations. For Lippmann and his defenders, the project consisted of abandoning the heliotropism of the People to put the individual back at the center of the art of governance.

In fact, *The Phantom Public*, published a decade before *The Good Society*, revealed an even more radical denial of the idea of the people: "Instead of being allowed to think realistically of a complex of social relations, we have had foisted upon us by various great propagative movements the notion of a mythical entity, called Society, the Nation, the Community." This can be explained by the historical context of the years immediately preceding the war. Then the governments of the People (Popular Front, fascism, and Nazism) were omnipresent and the tensions were as strong as Lippman's affirmation in 1927 that: "An opinion of the right and the wrong, the good and the bad, the pleasant and the unpleasant, is dated, is localized, is relative. It applies only to some men at some time in some place under some circumstances. Against this deep pluralism thinkers have argued in vain... We, however, no longer expect to find a unity which absorbs diversity. For us the conflicts and differences are so real that we cannot deny them and instead of looking for identity of purpose we look simply for an accommodation of purposes."

This assertion could finally only be an unconvincing, vague defense of representative democracy, in which the People is above all an entity represented by individuals with clear and limited functions. Because the affirmation of irreducible conflicts was the justificatory basis for world war, as a convinced democrat Lippmann could no longer make himself democracy's transmission belt. We will retain here this fundamental idea, unique to neoliberals, that radical pluralism doesn't accommodate the People. As a "mythical entity," the people cannot be the political center of gravity. Lippmann underlines this idea in *The Good Society*: "Thus the voice of the people speaking through their representatives has been regarded as the voice of God, and, when it seemed a little too preposterous to think of three or four hundred politicians as inspired, the even more preposterous claim has been advanced that some triumphant agitator contains within himself the mind and spirit and faith of great populations... The supposition that the rulers of a state can be fully representative of a whole society is a superstition."

For Lippmann, collectivism and the call to the people draws a continuum that logically leads to catastrophe. For the neoliberals, it is clear populism abolishes the distinction between democracies and dictatorships.

"Whether fascist, communist, or reformist, they recognize that liberalism is their great enemy, and they're right. The debate isn't among collectivist sects, but among all of them and liberalism." Lippmann quickly perceived the false populist messianism, and it is still true for neoliberals today that a positive totality can't drive a government. If a government wants to produce a stable and prosperous world, it must make liberty the limit and the hollow center of its power. But in order to understand the specific situation of French neoliberalism, we must again open the pages of French history.

In the general interwar crisis, neoliberalism wasn't the only cry of the epoch. Neo-socialism, neo-capitalism, neo-aestheticism, neo-realism, neo-syndicalism, neo-romanticism, neoliberalism, neo-Marxism, neo-colonialism, neo-protectionism, neo-impressionism, and neo-plasticism all bear witness to the urgency of regenerating and reinventing everything. Here, each one proclaims the death of its relatives. In the France of the interwar period, a persistent background melody would singularly mix and make itself heard alongside the new neoliberal refrain. In effect, that typically French fear of the crowd and the masses, a fear inaugurated by the *reaction* to the French Revolution, was superimposed on to the will to *not recognize* a people. This reaction is how the psychology of the crowd was born as the "science" of the apocalypse of the people.

When one looks at the French situation of the past two centuries, one observes an uninterrupted scene of the crowd and its folly. A long litany continued since the eighteenth century cautions us against the apocalyptic essence of the crowd. Let's listen to its most famous painter, Gustave Le Bon, sketch us a few of its most prominent traits: "Up to now these thoroughgoing destructions of a worn-out civilization have constituted the most obvious task of the masses. . . . History tells us, that from the moment when the moral forces on which civilization rested have lost their strength, its final dissolution is brought about by those unconscious and brutal crowds known, justifiably enough, as barbarians. . . When the structure of a civilization is rotten, it is always the masses that bring about its downfall."

Examples of the crowd's convulsive movements and its apocalyptic appearance abound, and the diffusion of an aesthetic of the crowd surpassed the narrow circle of a few notable paranoiacs. In *The Revolt of the*

Masses, José Ortega y Gasset, one among numerous prophets of apocalypse, develops a thesis that maintains that mass could not be reduced to class: "The mass is all that which sets no value on itself—good or ill—based on specific grounds, but which feels itself 'just like everybody,' and nevertheless is not concerned about it; is, in fact, quite happy to feel itself as one with everybody else."

As there is plebe in all classes, there is also mass in all classes. In *The Democratic Mystique* (1925), Louis Rougier, a disciple of Le Bon and Ortega y Gasset, more famous for his role in the New Right than his participation in the Walter Lippmann Colloquium and the first steps of "neoliberalism," speaks of the crowd in the same way as the people: "If the crowd combats the 'democratic mystique' as it was formulated by the ideologues of the Revolution. . . it is because it rests on this theological and mystical idea that the voice of the people is the voice of God, that none better than the people know how to discern their interests, and that men, of whom each in particular is subject to error, become infallible once they deliberate in an assembly, because then they receive, as Saint Augustine taught, the illumination of the Paraclete."

Lippmann and Rougier have both little and much to do with each other. In *Economic Mystiques* (1938), Rougier affirms the need to return to a neoliberal order, a "constructive liberalism" that coincides point by point with that of Lippmann's *The Good Society*. Rougier, an anti-Christian paganist, radical anti-Semite, and anti-Enlightenment conservative—and, paradoxically, through all this an anti-collectivist liberal—strangely speaks the same language as Lippmann, a former socialist, progressive liberal, and fervent defender of a "social," humanist liberalism. Rougier's lamentation explains how the roots of French neoliberal antipopulism diverge so far from that of his German and American comrades.

In France, neoliberalism has always been colored by its reverse excess—a profound distaste for the masses allied with a rhetorical—which is to say, catachretic—populism. This contradiction in terms is equally accompanied by an obsession with the "third way." In truth, the problem of French neoliberalism is that of a bourgeoisie haunted by historical compromise. As we are going to see, one would have to wait until the 1990s for the bourgeoisie to exorcise its past demons—the

Conseil national de la Résistance (National Council of the Resistance) and Gaullism. Continuing his intellectual interventions, Rougier affirms that the renunciation of liberalism leads to a catastrophe of civilization. He was also one of the originators of the famous French third way and of "historicized liberalism." In a 1938 article entitled "Return to Liberalism," he notes that, unlike strong and coherent systems like communism and corporate fascism, one reason for the fragility of liberal democracies resides in their precarious synthesis of two contradictory elements. On one hand, liberalism wants to present itself as the guarantor of individual liberties, personal initiative, and a free play of competition that naturally fixes the best prices. On the other hand, democracy is a political aberration in which the sovereign people choose their own path. In a long indictment of all forms of planning, Rougier supports the idea that liberal democracies, if they want to save themselves, must abandon the ideal of popular sovereignty in exchange for that of individual rights. This is how historicized liberalism was born. "Historicized," because for Rougier, as for Lippmann, the project didn't consist in falling back into a naïve and naturalizing version of liberalism. As Lippmann says in his chapter "The Debacle of Liberalism" (*The Good Society*):

> Having assumed that there was no law there, but that it was a natural God-given order, they (liberals) could only teach joyous acceptance or stoic resignation. Actually they were defending a system of law compounded from juristic remnants of the past and self-regarding innovations introduced by the successful and powerful classes in society. Moreover, having assumed away the existence of a system of man-made law governing the rights of property, contract, and corporation, they could not, of course, interest themselves in the question of whether this law was a good law, or of how it could be reformed or improved. The derision poured out upon the latter-day liberals as men who had become complacent is not unjustified. Though they were probably not more insensitive than other men, their minds stopped working.

If neoliberalism takes up liberty as a paradigm, it makes of it a "technique of governance." Liberty is constructed. It is the fruit of a permanent intervention. Neoliberals aren't absolutely against intervention—the matter consists in constructing the conditions of possibility for an economic liberty that must be the double, indeed the mirror, of political liberty.

Yet how can one think the question of sovereignty in political terms, if one renounces the people? This necessitates the invention of a non-apocalyptic social subject to save the idea of a majoritarian form. Neoliberal government acts in a fundamentally anti-apocalyptic mode. It conjures the people through making processes of individuation possible via the market. Through this, it produces the economico-social figure of the consumer. This figure in part owes its life to the political thought of Ludwig Von Mises, also the author of an adage Louis Rougier loved to cite: "every child that prefers one toy to another puts his ballot in a box from which the elected Captain of Industry appears." The consumer, this mass-individual qualified by a series of preferences, choices, and interests, replaces the people. Sovereignty is dissolved in the circle of society (capitalism). This is a people *for society.*

The true neoliberal takeover was to convert a theory of the market into a theory of human actions. Rather than operate as a rupture between Labor and Capital, neoliberal governance is the abolition of their very distinction. Democracy and market are confused and superimposed. Let's listen again to Ludwig von Mises speak about this in his treatise *Human Action* (1949):

> It would be more correct to say that a democratic constitution is a scheme made to assign to the citizens in the conduct of government the same supremacy the market economy gives them in their capacity as consumers. However, the comparison is imperfect. In political democracy, only the votes cast for the majority candidate or the majority plan are effective in shaping the course of affairs. The votes polled by the minority do not directly influence policies. On the market, however, no vote is cast in vain. Every penny spent has the power to work upon the processes of production.

As Michel Foucault showed in his course at the Collège de France on January 31, 1979, the peculiarity of neoliberal governmentality is that the economy is not simply a branch of national activity, but the productive activity of sovereignty and of the people:

> Let's say that in leaving people free to act, the German neo-liberal institution lets them speak, and to a large extent it lets them act because it wants to let them speak; but what does it let them say? Well, it lets them say that one is right to give them freedom to act. That is to say, over and above juridical legitimation, adherence to this liberal system produces permanent consensus as a surplus product, and, symmetrically to the genealogy of the state from the economic institution, the production of well-being by economic growth will produce a circuit going from the economic institution to the population's overall adherence to its regime and system.

Neoliberalism destitutes the people, unworks it and leaves it inoperative. It erects in exchange a consumer people, an anti-people whose catachresis is canceled out because the consumer is constructed as a real figure. An antipopulist people completes the circle. Enterprise would be this new power of composition that has now become society's place of veridiction. On February 21, 1979, Foucault said of neoliberalism, "it is not an economic government, (but) a government of society." The base unit of society is no longer the people but the enterprise and the individual-enterprise linked by the market: "Concretely, in this liberal society in which the true economic subject is not the man of exchange, the consumer or producer, but the enterprise, in this economic and social regime in which the enterprise is not just an institution but a way of behaving in the economic field."

A neoliberal government is one whose center is empty and whose sides are full of techniques. It acts not on a mythic totality but on the liberty of individuals. On one hand, liberty becomes a *technique of government*. On the other, the people are reduced to a series of competitions. No unity can be bestowed upon the diverse because there is no longer a center of gravity from which a foundation of truth and salvation can be drawn that neoliberalism can govern. If, in the nineties, in the face of the demolition of the USSR and the ebb of the idea of communism, neoliberals could delight in a hypothetical end of history, they had the hubris of believing they had divested capitalism of its apocalypse.

LANDSCAPE V: BECOME UNGOVERNABLE

Whispers reveal the present is unbearable and everywhere swells this diffuse sentiment that the world, from now on, will be an infernal reality. This should destroy once and for all the illusion that it's possible to live in peace with the holy law of catastrophe. The emotions raised by the sufferings and ambiguities of our inconsistent and "unredeemable" existences bring our generation to pose questions of final values that largely differ from those of the ultimate disciples of classical politics. For those of us who are young and who possess the feeling of having always lived under the reign of catastrophe, *the beginning is the end.*

For those of us who organize in France, the situation is paradoxical. According to Bruno Latour, "nothing in our muscles of French democrats prepares us. . . . We are mostly totally immobile and at once totally mobilized, like the choir of opera soldiers who sing at the top of their lungs, "Let's go, march!," without moving at all. . . . We stand still, boiling with indignation."

This is how "*En Marche*!" became Macron's victorious slogan during the last presidential elections. It was necessary for an "unfortunate" set of circumstances to bring him to power so that French bipartisanship, that old left-right alternation they had presented to us as the paragon of democracy, turn into parody. On one side, the Socialist Party drowned in the void of its contradictions and lies. On the other, the old conservative Republican right, unable to renew its reactionary political program, was hounded at its extremes by the fascist pressures of Marine Le Pen. And let's not forget the anachronistic candidate embodied in this Ancien Régime man, François Fillon. Classical politics à la française dies and pure neoliberalism makes its return. Under Macron's silly smile lies hidden that famous French third way. The idea of happiness he tries to sell us is the epitome of paradoxical hybridity—a mix of caresses toward the ancient, historic glory of France, economist technocracy doped up on *Big Data*, the governmentality of *soft powers* with police clubs, and a neoliberal mythology of the entrepreneurial *self-made man* hypostatized in a *startup* adventurer.

It is amusing to note, nevertheless, that the challenge to Macron didn't even wait for his arrival to power to set things in motion. In the spring of 2016, the movement against the Loi Travail reshuffled the cards of conflictuality for years to come.[1]

In Paris, in contrast to classical French social movements, the waves of anger didn't emerge through the initiatives of trade union confederations or the pompous protests of old, embittered trade unionists. In a kind of amusing dialectic, the movement was carried by those elements most available at the heart of the metropole. The first protests weren't the result of a call from the confederations, but an incidental conglomeration of Twitter users and Youtubers united under the hashtag "#werebetterthanthis" (#onvautmieuxqueça). In the first weeks of the movement, street conflictuality and riots were carried out by high school students who participated in blockades and completely autonomous protests. This heralded the great deluge with the simultaneous birth of the *cortège de tête*[2] and Nuit Debout (Up All Night) on March 31, 2016. Though they indicate two opposed hypotheses, these two mass events were nevertheless loaded with lines of flight. And this is a good thing for our party.

The cortège de tête wasn't merely the *visibilization strategy* of radical youth trying to exceed the unions' security forces in order to advance and get "stupidly caught up with the police." The forces of the movement of 2016 were lively to the extent they broke with French social movements' habitus and classical repertoire of action. To see more than just a handful of students and civil servants become active, one would have to wait until the month of April for the trade union confederations to finally decide to peer in on the battle. All those that passed up the trade union parade to take the head of the protest on March 31 did so because they no longer posed the question of their own legitimacy vis-à-vis that of the unions.

What confers on the event of the cortège de tête its force and radicality is that, for a time, a substantial group (sometimes ten thousand

1. The Loi Travail, or El Khomri law, was first presented to the French Parliament in February 2016. It was devised as a form of austerity to alter France's labor laws, making it easier to lay off workers and reduce certain types of employment compensations and payments.

2. *Cortège de tête* is an inversion of tête de cortège, a term that literally means "head of the procession," and that refers in this case to the often funereal union parade classically positioned at the head of the protest march. While cortège, from the Italian *corteggio*, reveals its aristocratic roots as a term derived from the somber rituals of the royal *corte*, or court, the linguistic undoing of this formula marks the way in which the tired ritual of the march itself was unworked through the efforts of radical youth to outflank the unions' parade and take the head of the march, detailed further in the account below.

people, as on June 14) no longer posed the question of ends before that of means. Through this, the mass of the cortège de tête neutralized those old couples of traditional opposition—negativity and positivity, critique and proposition, destruction and construction—and unfastened one of the linchpins of classical politics. For a time, even in the heart of Paris one could see spreading the contagion of taking sides.

The cortège de tête was nothing other than a long operation of subtraction, a machine that unworked the habitual story of what a classical protest should be (whose clear utterances, marking out a precise field of demands and determined objectives, neutralize the possibilities of giving any protest a proper name). The cortège de tête operated like a *tikkun*, a reparation of protest. The lost *technê* of the protesters was restored to them. Here "solidarity" was no longer a hollow slogan, a call, but a politics of immediate love. Medics, protesters, the masked, and unmasked all stood together to resist the attacks of the police. The outrageous slogan of the Confédération générale du travail (General Confederation of Labor, or CGT), "Or else it'll explode," was finally conjugated in the present tense.

The etymology of the word *apokálupsis* brings to light a tradition that is often forgotten by our contemporaries. The apocalyptic character of an event originally resides not in some sense of catastrophe but in the capacity to *reveal*. The apocalyptic character of the cortège de tête precisely *took hold* through a gesture that consisted in revealing, rather than contemplating or proposing. In this way, as hundreds were arrested and thousands were injured, a young generation noticed how ready power is to defend the metropolis and its infrastructures. The operation of the cortège de tête was destituent precisely in that it brought a new field of conflictuality directly to the heart of the protest and the metropole. The force of the cortège de tête endured through a capacity to announce resonant truths as well as a will to *always begin*. The choreography of the cortège de tête, which consisted of thousands taking the front of the protests in order to put themselves at its head by outflanking it, is the image of the birth of our generation. We shout out, in the cortège de tête, nothing else but this. It is true that, as moved as we are by an ardent desire for the contrary, we will not be able to dispense with destruction. We want to demolish what exists, not for the love of the rubble, but for the love of the paths that cross it. The positivity of the cortège de tête, if one desires to locate it, resides in a childish simplicity lodged entirely in our capacity to fuse together. A text published on June 22 on the site *Lundi Matin* articulated something similar:

> those who fight / those who chant / those who care / cortège de tête / our peopling / our propagation / human packs / and animal packs / proliferation / by contagion / by epidemic / on the field of battle / in the face of catastrophe / I already / await / the return / of the tête de cortège

In parallel with the event of the cortège de tête, Nuit Debout carried out its constituent effort. If one can see the cortège de tête as the act of a partisan body that refused the political and police operations of subjectification, Nuit Debout, on the other hand, with its cries for self-transparency, radical democracy, and a flight forward in unending research on political subjectification, nearly incarnated the opposite. In this light, it doesn't come as a surprise that the general assembly soon stumbled over the question of the people.

There is always, in the mythic invocation of the people, a constituent tendency. It is the will to take oneself into account as a collective subject with stable, precise demands—almost *realist* demands, one could say. To revisit Laclau, it is also this constituent tendency that encloses the unlimited signifier of "the society" in constructing its antagonism of demands. It consists in this famous "constituent power" that guaranteed the realization of charters, constitutions, and programs. And then there is the people-plebe, this thing that escapes categories, "is in all classes" and evades every political fixity. These two antagonistic visions seem to have crossed the whole sequence of the movement of struggle over the Loi Travail. On one side, the constituent people (that of Nuit Debout, the unions and a certain fraction of the left-wing of the movement); on the other side, this *mixture*, with ever-moving boundaries and no expectations with regard to the political game in play. The cortège de tête.

Again and again, at the very heart of the cortège de tête, a banner came to stand for the importance of this new horizon of expectation shared by a large number of protesters. It owed its beauty to a simple, concise utterance: "Become Ungovernable." The emergence of mottos and slogans is always more significant than the appearance of a certain logic or strategy. It also represents a certain partition of the sensible, which, spreading and taking on global proportions, adapts to local sensibilities. For instance, the utterance "all power to the Soviets" resounded throughout the entire world by way of example. From Germany to Russia, passing through Italy and Spain, the utterance was invested in and took on meaning in different ways. The gestures inscribed in it indicated the destitution of bourgeois power and the creation of a new order, indexed to an other myth-people. Could we suspect that "ungovernable" will undergo the same trajectory? Could it establish, globally, a partition of the sensible, a political vision of the future? Not at present, but a good number of signs lead us to believe that its diffusion is not accidental. From Brazil to the United States, from France to England and Italy, this phrase exceeds its simple slogan-like character. It no longer conjures a mythic totality and also breaks with the multi-centenary paradigm according to which getting organized is governing. "Ungovernable" doesn't give a name to unprecedented practices—as were the councils in their time—but to a relation from self to self that no longer passes through the people as the place of political truth. In this way, refusing the notion of government at the heart of democratic states is in some way refusing the principle of classical politics itself, and it is by way of destitution that the power of this utterance operates.

Metanarratives are dead, and each new fashionable cultural product reminds us there is nothing innocent in this world. Series, films, and contemporary novels give us the description of a world where everything is made of gold and yet already entirely spoiled. We are linked to the objects and beings that surround us by an intimate familiarity. This reflects the sparks of the universal catastrophe. Confronted by the accomplished reign of mutilated life at every scale, socialism has abandoned the utopic terrain, while the extreme Left no longer knows how to pose the question of life (Let it bang its head against the wall of authenticity). The question, in fact, has often been poorly posed. If we haven't given up in the face of the endless apocalypse of our time, we should envision the turn *life actually takes* and not naively the one we think it should take. The aggregation of our forces along a *via negationis* takes shape against the "bad" arrangement of the world. It takes shape against our catastrophe, against both what wears away the very possibility of a good and desirable life as much as the uses incumbent upon such a life. As "wrong life cannot be lived rightly," "ungovernable" embodies this new ethical negativism. It is an utterance with no concessions to the present. It is a motto that, extracting itself from the crumbling old regime of promise, comes to determine possible positive contents—here and now—by the negative of negation.

What is at play here is the refusal to pose certain questions, namely those of promise and salvation. This also entails the abandonment of the question that framed the revolutionary tradition's old problematic: "Who is the people and how can we erect it into a self-government?" Is this then an operation of inversion or the transvaluation of values? It's not one or the other, but an abandonment.

Liberty as the removal of determinant conditions cedes to liberty as the destitution of determinant conditions to replace them with reparation and the refusal of removal. This is the case even in the most corrupt places. This can take the form of refusing the destruction of a neighborhood where one lives, or of an abandoned place or park, as during the movement of Taksim in 2013, of a valley like the Val di Susa, a wooded countryside like that of Notre-Dame-des-Landes, or of a sacred territory like Standing Rock.

If we summarize an epoch by its paradoxes, ours is that what is called "our way of life" also coincides with a dynamic of assured self-destruction. By accepting the rules of life today, one returns to fading away in an unprecedented feeling of solitude. Nevertheless, the current global sequence attests to the multiplication of attempts at shattering this paradox.

Being ungovernable, from this point of view, is being irreducibly anchored to a negative dynamic. At the same time, through a deeper, clandestine critique of the West, what is ungovernable *positively renews* through its refusal of the multi-millenary machine of government. This machine has spread and naturalized itself to the point of constituting biological life itself. "Men have governed from time immemorial," they tell us. In this light, one must soberly revisit the words of Bataille. "Secretly or not, it is necessary to become other, or else cease to be." What in 1936 seemed a mystic gnosis today offers the figure of a commonplace. "The world or nothing."

How? What does it mean to be governed? It means to be conducted, one way or another. In fact, all social figures are there to say what to do or what not to do, how to do it, in what context, by what means and forms. Professors, doctors, police, judges, all manner of administrators, social workers, activity leaders, salespeople—the object of each one is a subject to govern: students, patients, delinquents, the administrated, children, and clients. There is no social relation that does not include some manner of conducting, of governing. It is also the very ethos of management, a figure so diffuse and omnipresent in our time. Elections are the re-actualization of this principle at a higher level. Each candidate participates in them with a demonstration regarding his or her capacity to conduct men.

What is left for us, orphans of the great political projects of the governance of humans and things, projects that crystallized promises of better times? An incredible luck, in fact, still remains for us—the opportunity to know that the refusal of whatever "government" again facilitates an unprecedented overcoming. Abandoning the classical frame of politics and the substratum of relations between the governing and the governed liberates us from the multi-millenary concern that we must, as a political animal, govern, represent, manage—in short, produce an arduous and painful form of common life. Of this, Nuit Debout offered a terrible foretaste.

Whoever takes the side of government takes the side of endless apocalypse. Whoever takes the side of the ungovernable takes the side of abandoning finality for reparation and means. Reparation against eschaton without end and the ungovernable against partisans of governmentality—this will likely be the major issue of the coming political conflicts. The failures of Syriza in Greece, Podemos in Spain, Mélenchon and his *insoumis* in France, Sanders in the United States, and Corbyn in Great Britain—the failures of all these left populists who have risen up against the eschaton without end reveal their inability to understand that the political now resides in the apocalyptic itself.

It is true that neoliberalism has driven politics back and left only a hollow center. The place of the people is empty and easily taken. Anyone can take it, even a neoliberal like Macron. Immanence is local. The only plane of consistency on which to operate, act, and initiate something requires attracting toward oneself otherwise elusive finalities. Jean-Baptiste Fressoz gives the name "the sublime of the Anthropocene" to that ecstasy and fear inspired by the apocalyptic work of man, formerly attributed to the terrible forces of nature that prompted an ecstatic feeling of powerlessness. In the face of this sublime, taking part is no longer constructing the party of the people to come. Instead, *to repair is to now destroy that which binds us to the end of the world*. There is an urgent need to connect questions of building, inhabiting, and thinking to those of combat, according to a planetary plane of consistency capable of repairing as much as destroying. Standing Rock, the ZADs, Taksim, and the cortège de tête are all acts of *tikkun*. In their confrontation with governmentality and its material infrastructures, they plunge to the very roots of the problem.

Here, after all, we only complete the prediction made by an old prophet in a commentary on the apocalyptic twilight of the Paris Commune, written in the form of an ultimate *revelation*: "The next attempt of the French revolution will be no longer, as before, to transfer the bureaucratic-military machine from one hand to another, but to *smash* it" (Marx, April 12, 1871).

RUIN, FURY, FRAGMEN-TATION

Catalans, One More Effort!

They sentenced me to twenty years of boredom
For trying to change the system from within
I'm coming now, I'm coming to reward them...
—Leonard Cohen, "First We Take Manhattan"

"The rapidity with which the insurgents organized themselves into a kind of army would have seemed remarkable in any other country that wasn't Catalonia. But the Principality had a long tradition of collective action. During the civil wars of the fifteenth century, Catalans had developed very effective "syndicates." In the sixteenth and at the beginning of the seventeenth century... little time was necessary for the news of armed conflict to travel from one village to another, principally because it was a common practice to sound the parish bells each time help was needed. During this first week of May, the bells rang through all the valleys, from Sant Feliu to Tordera. The province took up arms and rose up."
—John H. Elliott, *The Revolt of the Catalans* (1598–1640)

To Pablo Milano, to friends, after two years of sustaining the pain of your absence.

PART I: FURY

1

In Catalonia anything could have happened. Maybe.

Psychic energies and the capacity for self-organization were present. There was also an immense desire to *interrupt the present disaster* and start again. But start what? This is not clear either. Though what was absolutely unclear was *who would take the initiative.*

In any case, "big and little captains" weren't going to form within their political chess games. These games seemed intelligent at first, although they belonged precisely to this class of cursed *indecision* that is the motor of catastrophe. They entail the tepidity and exhaustion familiar to metropolitan life, familiar to the absence of just fury. Juvenile fury, *iuvenis furor*? Georges Dumézil pointed out the ancient tradition of many Italian towns "that proclaim as their founders a band of *iuvenes* led by an animal consecrated to Mars." Ever since a prehistory that still beats not only etymologically within us, fury, *at once physical and supernatural*, has been associated in the West with conserving or obtaining true independence.

2

The most horrible moment was when there was not only no desire to call for blockading everything—which would have demonstrated *de facto* as well as *de jure* a total independence—but also an attempt, even among militants, to justify the paralysis by citing the state and armed forces' *determination to be violent*. "*Natros som gent de pau*," they say.[1] We who? Are these the same provincial and mountain-dwelling *Catalans* in the face of whose providential ferocity and intensity that, as Niccolò Machiavelli recalls that when the Borgia Pope was elected, in Rome they exclaimed "*Oh no, i Catalani!*"

Cursed be the excessively pacifist, for, as has been said, *their cruel caution will bring them a threatening absence of peace.*

Such being the nature of things, the ambition to found a sovereign State seems ridiculous, if State is the monopoly of violence and if sovereign is the one who decides the state of exception. No exceptional moment nor decisive confrontation. It is true that what the *Govern* didn't want was to unleash a conflict whose breadth and intensity would allow the situation to slip out of their hands. A situation of intense malaise, a diffuse hatred, and the streets filled with people. Though it is sad to say, as is the case in every culturally bourgeois stratum, there was a desire for *negotiation*. And I am not talking about the independentist "movement," I am talking about the organized forces at its heart, from the various parties and associations to the radical neo-social democracy of the Candidatura d'Unitat Popular (Popular Unity Candidacy, or CUP)—whose parliamentary tactics have turned into

1. "We are a peaceful people."

an essence ever since the good heads they have in parliament got stuck like flies to the institutional spiderweb. It has been a long time since one spoke of the bourgeoisie as the argumentative class *par excellence*. What has happened is that the CUP weren't confronted with a bourgeoisie but a State, "the coldest of cold monsters." A State only pursues its own conservation, especially against its own people.

3

What is it, then, that has captured or fascinated so many friends in Catalonia? Since the referendum drew closer and the first arrests were made, it seemed the regime of 1978 could burst into pieces. Thousands of people, many of whom weren't independentists, flooded the streets, feeling alive and shattering their solitude. As one of the political certainties of the epoch, self-organization in local committees proliferated. Blockade, sabotage, occupation, attacks on police, and, finally, the appearance of positively delirious and anomic places of encounter, all form part of an incomplete constellation of the epoch. In any case, after the sadness of the past years, in which the ebb of the cycle of struggles has been paid for by a multitude of suicides and the intensification of the reign of a diffuse politico-toxicomania, something is something. Not strategy, but something.

4

Fascination with the masses. Finally the masses in the street! This strange People to whom one makes it known one doesn't belong.

On October 3, in the afternoon, with Catalonia blockaded and the streets of Barcelona full of protesters, we joined the group coming from the neighborhoods of Santa Eulalia, Sants and the Poble Sec. A pack in multiplicity together crossing the metropolis wherever it wanted, calling out "*Els carrers seran sempre nostres!*".[2] We arrived at the limit of the city's *zona alta*, the Avenida Diagonal, where we could no longer advance. At one point, I went to find a restroom and look for water. I had to go really far. The composition of the mass I traversed also carried independentist flags. But, in their way of carrying themselves, they didn't look like they wanted the same kind of independence. I went back to the pack of protesters, but I felt

2. "Whose streets? Our streets!"

infinitely strange, so I said goodbye and walked home, spending more than an hour crossing streets full of nationalist flags.

I will mention that, at noon, after some of us left the group that came from the neighborhood, worn out by the desire of a few friends to direct everything, I accompanied a group of young protesters in the city's center, and went to see an Israeli friend. There we crossed paths with some anarchists from Andalusia that had come to Barcelona and were accompanying a group from the Confederación Nacional del Trabajo (National Confederation of Labor, or CNT). My Israeli friend was furious. She gave us a monumental reprimand. "In my country we have already seen all this, we've seen it for a long time!" she said. "Grandmothers facing off with groups of police and then hugging other police, their police." "Nationalist flags disguising emancipatory ideals, they should all end up in the toilet! I've seen horrible messages on Facebook for days, people posting photos of hugs with cops and flirting with supremacism, saying: "We Catalans *will* make a State like God demands." And what people has been more oppressed than the Jewish people? And look what's happened! You want a State? Are we crazy or what? Don't we fight against everything this means?" What she had read in the situation was what all those who were participating from a desire to change everything refused to recognize. Fragmentation.

PART 2: FRAGMENT TO FRAGMENT

> *"It is time, most of all, to discover in presence itself the material and 'historical' presence of the possible. Revolution starts in the body."*
>
> —Giorgio Cesarano, *Survival Manual*

5

When I returned to Italy, I devoured Wilhelm Reich's *The Mass Psychology of Fascism*. What I had seen in Barcelona wasn't exactly "fascism," but indeed the remains of an overlooked petty bourgeoisie.

The question to which Reich was trying to respond in 1933 was not that of why those who have hunger rob or why the exploited strike, but why a majority of the hungry don't rob and a majority of the exploited don't go on strike. Today the most interesting part of his analysis is that, in the first place, the petty bourgeoisie's special social position, *always in competition with everything and everyone*, makes it unable to get organized and create experiences of communality and profound solidarity and form an other world in the face of power. The result is that its desire for power degenerates into a desire for safety and protection, turning it toward the leader or the *nation*. Most of all, the petty bourgeoisie won't make alliances with proletarian strata because what it fears most, after all, is *proletarianization*. In second place, Reich notes that the determinant factor in breaking with reactionary "character formation," anchored in an archaic, proprietary and despotic patriarchy, resides in forms of life—in the thousands of little gestures that make everyday life an open place of conspiracy and combat, encounter and communality, or instead turn it into an open-air prison of sadness. Revolutionaries, Reich notes, have entrusted pamphlets and slogans with a transformation of *life*, while immense sections of the working class kept getting married, buying themselves "bourgeois bedroom suites," going for a walk on Sundays in "elegant" clothing, or barricading their houses for fear of thieves (the neighbors). Today one no longer gets "elegant" to go out on Sunday, but on Friday, on Saturday, or on any other day. The bedroom is now included in the "house," whose desirous image bombards those on the sofa of each house, each night, on television. The image of the successful boss is projected onto the big multinational or the *startup*, according to the premise of a life converted into an exhausting enterprise, *always in competition with everything and with everyone*. The generalization of the feeling that one lives among enemies has led to the proliferation of the domestic security industry, producing ever more sophisticated locks and crossbars.

Patriarchal love has been divided between its paradoxical overcoming in the universal capitalist community of the therapeutic Great Void, which Cesarano already analyzed in 1974. Patriarchal love is the purveyor of narcissistic disaster, plotting out a degenerate persistence in stories that end in femicide, in family resignation that makes everyone unhappy, and in the not insignificant contemporary fragments of conservatism and neo-fascism.

6

The independentist movement has been, in relation to the gathering of fragments of world, a real multiplicity. Yet in the massive, coordinated figures and longing-for-State of its annual televised gatherings, it has been, since 2012, the great social movement of a petty bourgeoisie whose decomposition underwent a qualitative leap precisely in these last years—a leap of impoverishment. A planetary petty bourgeoisie, as has been said, strangely galvanized as a mass, with an exploded content of values, expresses in its own instability the *fragmentation of the world*. In fact, the mass independentist movement knows it is not only a fragment of the population of Catalonia, but first and foremost that it is internally fragmented—ungovernable—hence the countless viral messages full of suspicion as the tension rose: *"A les 21 h. tots a casa. Qui es quedi al carrer* és *un provocador!" "Atenció, ha passat un cotxe negre amb policies infiltrats. Cap resposta." "Som gent de pau".*[3]

7

The experience of a petty bourgeois existence is generally much more intense in the heart of metropolitan areas because of their conditions of rootlessness and isolation.

In a world marked by physical and metaphysical deterioration, petty bourgeois existence isn't so much defined by a strict identity of values as by the fear of losing a *differential*, relatively secure social position.

The dissolution of clear social identities (bourgeois with a top hat, proletarian with a work jumpsuit and cap, or petty bourgeois shopkeeper) led to the elaboration of figures like the anonymous man or Bloom. Between opportunism and narcissism, apathy and emptiness, both of these figures are defined by a radical ambivalence. They, being nothing, could be anything. The son of a paramilitary of the Civil Guard could become the most determined armed insurgent.

It is true such figures are-there, they exist and even dominate the Westernized landscape. They also *share flesh*, however, in continuous bifurcations or internal polarities, with petty bourgeois existences.

3. "Everyone home by 9 p.m. Those who stay out are provocateurs! Attention! A black car with police infiltrators just passed by. Don't respond! We are a peaceful people."

What I want to say is that, while impoverished—and for this reason more dangerous—the petty bourgeois way of existing still endures. It subsists, as elsewhere amidst the epoch's remains, in the metropolis, and as a more than minor fragment of the independentist movement.

The best environment in which this way of life crystallizes and prospers, blocking other singular becomings, is the *nationalist* State.

The petty bourgeoisie is a fragment of world whose patriarchal-proprietary *affects* of interest, isolation, desire for order, fear of chaos, and panic at multiplicity and alterity make it prone to authoritarian and neo-fascist turns: desire for police, desire for State. The universal capitalist community of the therapeutic Great Void, in battle for decades with the patriarchal family as a stronghold of powerful bonds, is coerced by a social-democratic powerlessness—itself no less proprietary, isolated, interested, desirous for order and fearful of chaos—to fulfill the most ridiculous role of the epoch. These pacified petty bourgeois ways are always subject to a threatening absence of peace.

8

Petty bourgeois affects crystallize as roots in rootlessness, as an existential link with a space-time that is a perfect non-place for any metropolis. This entails an absence made of velocity that, integrated into global capitalist mobilization, can rise up in any moment against oneself, as a *monster* that casts you out without further thought.

This is what happens today to thousands of families in the *independentist* Barcelona, yet without, for all that, unleashing a *just devastation*. This would be the case if the inhabited place were a differentiated fabric of links between the land and techniques, animals and plants, humans and spirits, even *genius loci*. But things aren't like that. The thousands of new deluxe real estate properties that have arrived like a plague in every neighborhood seem unaware of their eventual destiny as fuel for the fire, material to be used in an imprudent agitation that, if it doesn't qualitatively silence a trail of explosions, will have participated in its pacification. Just as the unions and Communist parties administered the workers' defeats of the 1970s.

When the same being who was about to leave, resigned to a law in which she was *interested*, decides to stay instead, and get organized and fight, she is *altering her affects*. She is affirming her risk and limiting her possibility, yet enriching it in the same movement. This being finds in her presence plebeian forces that exist in each body and is ready to secede, with fury, with a *just violence* Luisa Muraro would say, as part of a fragment of world whose intensity contemplates its own perfection.

PART 3: FRAGMENTATION

> *"Tyrants are never born in anarchy. You only see them rise up in the shadow of the law or by seeking shelter in it."*
>
> —Marquis de Sade, *Juliette*

9

Perhaps what has occurred in Italy recently offers a radical example that elucidates the fragmentation of the world. In Macerata, a small city in the center of the country, Innocent, a Nigerian drug dealer, allegedly murdered and carved up an 18-year-old Italian girl who had just shot up heroin. They found her in pieces in garbage bags, and in Innocent's apartment an axe and traces of blood. Days later, a 32-year-old fascist went for a ride downtown with his glock. He shot at several African immigrants, resulting in six injured, one seriously. The key, however, is not in the extremes (fascist, murderer, drug dealer) but in the mediocrity. It is in what the fascist's lawyer told the *Corriere della Sera* when he said he was surprised by the infinite demonstrations of support for the gunman, not only on the Internet but on the streets of the same small city where the acts occurred.

Each degenerately offensive gesture of the Right, and uselessly compassionate gesture of the Left, diffracts chains of hatred and resentment that only the Right takes up as *different orientations to existence*. This is existential difference that is not worth discussion. Between these orientations it is only possible to maintain one's distance, *compose oneself*, or fight.

Each degenerately offensive gesture of the Right and uselessly conciliatory progressive gesture appeals to a unity no one desires to claim and whose deterioration as such is clearly evident. Modern sovereign unity is a *unity of terrible life*. In crisis as a form of government, catastrophe perpetuates itself as the threat of catastrophe, chaos as the final refuge against chaos. The false becomes a moment of the false beating in the heart. This is why appeals to *popular* as much as *national* unity only provoke more malaise, more anguish over fragmentation, more misery, more massacre, and more hypocrisy.

Among the massive response that took the form of multiple antifascist protests in Italy, the offensive character of Piacenza measured up to the *plebeian hatred* the epoch exudes.

10

Fragmentation, as Josep Rafanell i Orra reveals in *Fragmenter le monde*, appeals to a link with the place where one lives and a bond among the beings, mechanisms, constructions, and spirits that populate it.[4] It appeals to a politics of encounter and communal inquiry as well as to travel from place to place as a form of revolutionary becoming. In Sufism, the shock caused by the encounter with Allah—with *what is*—is explained through the experience of the voyage. When a voyage is being together without any other task but being, it's always a voyage at once external and internal. It never leaves things the same.

All the constituent mania and calls for popular unity appeal to the same *unity of catastrophe* that *is* the metropolis, as the culminating expression of governmental modernity. Unity, under a State that *is* the economy—of abstract spaces, non-places, sad work, sensible, idiotic screens, slaves, and masters united in alienation.

11

Both before and after a supposed national independence, Catalonia already explodes in fragments, articulated among each other by way of governmental prostheses. Half of the population does not want to live under the Spanish state, the other half doesn't want to do so in an independent Catalonia, and a nameless remainder remains without a voice. Fragmentation. Yet these fragments can exist perfectly just as they are, supporting each other. Their earthly and communal "composability," their openness but also substantiality and determination, will define their

4. *Fragmenter le monde*, or *Fragment the World*, was published by Editions Divergences in 2018.

durability. Communes, and not States, are what some revolutionaries intend to experiment with in the East as in the West.

Calls to popular unity don't resolve the matter of "incomposability"—the impossibility of composing an articulation—with the Francoist and neo-fascist fragments. This is resolved through maintaining distances or fighting. Civil war is not the extreme limit of political life as much as its origin.

12

The perception of a fragmented world has collided with the dogma of unity. In spite of all the intense communality that is still *truly* unfolding in so many Republican Defense Committees, local committees, and little places, my objection to the general triumphalism and enthusiasm was found in the *mode of presence* at the heart of the autumn conflict. On one hand, a part of the autonomous and libertarian group—not insurrectionists—had fallen into *mass* fascination, and their experience as encounter and experimentation was evidently positive. At least some among the most active, however, did this without trying to compose a *differentiated position from within the situation*. Instead the reverse happened, and some became activists of the governmental triumvirate. Being captured by mass enthusiasm, in the absence of a proper position, was already demolished in a consistent way in the "messianic" *April Theses*. On the other hand, the insurrectionists' critique was clearly sterile: This doesn't have anything to do with us, they only want a petty bourgeois State. The *strategic* position suggested that, participating from inside, without letting oneself be marginalized, it didn't make sense to assist a movement determined by citizenist forms. On the contrary, it was the moment to make way for neighborhood self-organization; to take a step aside and a somersault forward; to travel around in order to meet intelligent people and groups; to try to compose a force of action and enunciation; to compose combinations of differences eager to confront the institutional framework; to compose combinations of differences that would engage in thinking and interpreting, and take the initiative in precise moments and places. But this wasn't possible.

PART 4: RUIN

"This nocturnal tenacity, this recurrent appearance of underworlds, this universe of souls in constant danger was like a lifeblood to the trunk of the great rebellions."

—Antonio García de León, *Resistencia y utopía*

13

One of the problems that permeates the situation is an obsession with the slogan "*unitat popular*," or "popular unity." Today popular unity isn't given and doesn't materialize with the magic of words. This is the *populist* program, which illusorily divides the population by articulating conflicts around profoundly mythical feelings, like the homeland, thus creating a We and a They that propels a left-wing candidate, who sooner than later will be trapped in the institutional framework. "Hegemony without hegemony," as they have theorized in Brazil. Impotence. The only popular unity is the *unity in devastation*, as Ortega y Gasset pointed out, according to the term's etymology, and as the Invisible Committee has reminded us. What does it mean to call for popular unity when you've only received ten percent of the votes? I will tell you what it means. It means submitting to the initiative of a *Govern* that only wanted *voting* and negotiation.

What the situation required and still requires isn't popular unity but *strategic difference*. In Italy, in 1977, a concept of *difference-action* was elaborated. A multiplication of differences and initiatives that deepen the destruction of sadness and the reclaimed rupture of solitude. The differentiation of strategic offensives avoids marginalization and intensifies situations. It makes them resound and propels them as far as possible in order to start, in the next situation, from an ever-higher level. It is the intensity of these bifurcations that elevates the level of conflicts and not consensus, which flattens them out instead. Instead of such a branching out, however, there is just a *waiting* and returning. Waiting in hopes one reaches a level of unity that in fact in this way one can never reach, and coming back again and again and again to this assembly of lead, populated by activists hunting for their own cybernetic reputation instead of hungering after a common ungovernable potential.

14

After the Spanish state classified throwing rocks and Molotov cocktails as terrorism in the 1990s through a process that tended to equate Basque separatists Euskadi Ta Askatasuna (ETA) with the entire population, a wave of dogmatic pacifism destroyed militant university students. Rolando D'Alessandro analyzed this well. The resulting impotence catapulted too many intelligent people toward institutional careers. And it is only from this place that popular unity makes sense, the place of governing.

Beyond repeatedly trying to constitute, each one from their own corner, the new great unitary historical Subject in a world of ruins, it should instead be time to compose planes of consistency in which differences and fragments of world could manage to reverberate among each other, each one expressing in its own way forces determined to finish with a world of lies. This could actually be the "independence to change everything," without its hope of government.

Hope, especially hope in the State, is the perfect path toward insignificance.

15

The messages full of resentment that still flood social networks today attest to the fact that both recovering the future and escaping from the field of rubble of the Spanish state undoubtedly were and are some of independentism's biggest desires.

The objective of independence was to escape a ruin that, as psychoanalysis has suggested, one always self-deceptively thinks is outside oneself.

Creating a State is not going to save us from the present catastrophe. Have we heard about the oceans, the mass extinction underway, the Anthropocene? Have we heard about quantitative easing and the bubble economy that drowns the rich in dollars and ruins those from below? Have we heard about the world war that extends from Pakistan to beyond the African Atlantic? Have we heard about the war of counterinsurgency against the entire Mexican people and all of Central America? Are we stupid or what? The whole world is a ruin, captained by lunatics like Donald Trump, Vladimir Putin, and Kim Jong-un.

Ruins are meaningful fragments, as Walter Benjamin said in *The Origin of German Tragic Drama*. It so happens that, in a world in which power resides in infrastructures (power being *the being whose existence prevails*), ruins aren't so much old stones and beautiful columns as us. Ruins are humans, trees, fish, bacteria, mushrooms, and insects; ruins are the living beings that circulate amidst the excess of metropolitan environments made of cement and iron, plastic and silicon.

16

In an unusually clear way, the psychic energy that nourished autumn's Catalan revolt was electrified by a mythic feeling, a national feeling.

The fact that a strong sentimental potential existed is evident, beyond the smiles of ecstatic faces that made front pages across Europe, in the arguments referencing *the family* made by so many last-minute Catalan independentists: My grandmother didn't speak Spanish, my aunt suffered under Francoist repression, my mother. . . . In the family, profound affects of the sentimental unite with the mythic. The mythic smashes clocks and watches, linking us to *tenacious nocturnal beings, souls in constant danger, netherworlds*, histories of struggle and rebirth in which what dies in an individual changes life. The epiphany of an alterity made common in revolt.

17

Although a *rebellious* fragment certainly exists in Catalan independentism, it is minoritarian, and even more minoritarian when it comes to rejecting revolt. As the *nationalist desire for a State*, one can find the national mythic feeling within the contents of the culture of death and the Right that Furio Jesi analyzed brilliantly. We follow him from here, writing about the characteristics of the culture of the Right:

> The culture in which the past is a sort of homogenized paste that can be shaped and given form in the most useful way. It is that culture in which a religion of death, or of the exemplary dead, prevails. It is the culture that declares that indisputable values exist, indicated by capital letters: Tradition and Culture, most of all, but also Justice, Liberty, and Revolution. A culture, in short, that is made of authority and mythological certainty about the name of knowing, teaching,

> commanding, and obeying. Most of our cultural heritage, and, in fact, also that of those who today don't want to be right-wing, is a cultural residue of the right."

As national and not internationalist—internationalism today can only mean inter-communalism—independentism has functioned as a "mythological machine" that returns to an exemplary past, an empty paste, settled in itself. It is the purview of a Catalonia that, interpreted by an elite, requires and imposes a *unitary* projection toward the future. There are also obligatory behaviors, determined by the affects of those who find security and protection in the nation and chief: pacifism, listening to the leader, defending institutions, etc.

18

We have let the mythic potential of revolutionary internationalism be snatched up because of our fear of the technified myths of Nazism and fascism. The human being isn't only *rational*, but also mythic. History and myth, adult and savage, life and death coincide in the being that risks itself—in gatherings, listening, travel, and love. Images full of an abysmal sentimental potential proliferate in each human existence, becoming sensible truth—far from a power-hungry technification that instrumentalizes them—when they are inseparable from a form of life that resists.

The same independentist friends with whom I spoke about all this the other day were schizophrenically divided by their national mythological machine. The mythological machine, whose function one imagines as combinatory, in fact internally divides hopelessly. If, on one hand, they fervently defended each one of the false steps of the *adult* movement, on the other they showed me, late at night with fascination, *savage* rap and trap videos that speak of the Mad Max world of neighborhoods in ruins, guns, and violence. Perhaps the friends from *El Sobresalto* best intuited this ambivalence, putting *Yung Beef* and *La Vanguardia*'s Enric Juliana on the same offensive plane. Both the hatred of the plebes (dictated by justice), as much as their calm (which knows how to interrupt time between miniscule wonders) want to live on. As one knows, a mythological machine is only dismantled by *destroying the bourgeois conditions of life that make it possible.*

The trap kids already know they live among ruins, they know that we ourselves are the epoch's ruins. This is the reason for the hatred and violence they distill, as well as the strength of the bonds they pursue—the short-circuiting of the metropolis's neutralization of affects. The ruins are maintained as ruins, frozen and exhibited in museums, in a frozen world where death opposes life lived as a long anguish. In a tempered world, full of creative ability that knows how to burn and in which death is the enigmatic heart of life, ruins have always been freely used to support fragments of world.

19

Catalonia is an exemplary sign of the ruin that everywhere devastates the planet, especially an old Europe full of reactionary tics. The collapse continues and demands an ample destitution of the present. Experiments are also underway, although even among them a hell can also prosper. Pablo committed suicide without even letting us know. The act of his gesture can't be reduced to this, but our lack of attention and determination is inextricably linked to the dangers of the institutionalization of autonomous structures. This allows us to obtain things at the price of losing vibrancy, calm, attention to our surroundings and a disposition to travel. Together.

It hurts to constantly see the repetition of plans that can barely grasp experiences already dying in the cold. "We have to do something" and "at least we are doing something" are two phrases that denote inertia more than attention or strategic intelligence. How do we compose a *good life*? What are we looking for? What are we attacking, both within ourselves and elsewhere? Availing ourselves of structures isn't enough. We easily forget our being ruins of time, whose art of composition is opposed to the art of government, as well as to that of micro-bureaucracy, a disgraceful art that "has only produced monsters," as one revolutionary said.

In the face of congealed models of the collective—"That's a task for the communication group," "Committees!," "Why doesn't anyone come to the administration meeting?"—anguished responses to the catastrophe of urgency, we would instead do better by paying attention to what the situation brings. The same initiative can be disastrous in one moment or favorable in another. And if this life of capitalist shit has taught us something, it's that if someone is always busy, they can never dedicate themselves to what they love.

Paying attention to what happens and learning to dispossess oneself—and not only of blueprints or plans—requires an inner discipline and trust we lack. Paying attention to what happens, sharpening one's sensibilities and refining one's perceptions in the deepening of rifts that already exist. Tearing up the infrastructural threads of governance that maintain the unitary, continual catastrophe. Filling the air with unheard-of harmonies. Communism. The experience of silence. What is the task? What is its stillness? What is its fury? What is our gift? And how do we inhabit the interruption of time?

A schizoid mythological machine exists in our collectives and in each one of us, sadly separating our being savage children from our knowing-how-to-be adult. Destituting the bourgeois conditions of life that keep this machine functioning means destituting this separation. The end of the guilty party, the end of sadness in activity.

Between Catalonia and Lombardy
February 2018

GREETINGS FROM THE PENINSULA

At the place where the Adriatic and the Ionian meet, Quod opens the laptop and starts to type. Somewhere else, between different time zones, Libet grabs the phone and starts to answer.

Quod: I thought about what you asked me yesterday, and we should spend some time on it. In the end, populism is one of those terms whose use by the media leads to its perversion, a mystification of its. . .

Libet: It's not easy to define a word of such common use, the only adequate method is the logical-historical one: to reconstruct the biography of an idea, of an event, of a word.

Q: With all of our evidence, populism is an ethical-political movement that arose in the second half of the nineteenth century, more or less simultaneously, in imperial Russia and in the American Midwest.

L: Right, the Russian populism of the Narodniki, alongside the American populism of the farmers' struggle against the disruption of the agricultural market by the introduction of railroads.

Q: Even going back to the beginning, it can't escape a substantial dose of indeterminacy: the word "populist" in Russian has a spectrum of meanings that includes any behavior, from a revolutionary terrorist to a mild-mannered Slavophile philanthropist.

L: It seems to me that this word, very much used in our time, is a residue that explains nothing.

Q: What makes the indeterminacy irreversible is the absence of intellectual heirs capable of referring to populism and defending its experience. Populism has been defeated and the winners imposed, as usual, the derogatory meaning.

L: In Latin America, in the thirties and forties, it meant a certain form of governance that established a relation of direct embodiment between a people and its leader, bypassing forms of parliamentary representation.

Q: Well, there was the "twenty-first century socialism" according to Hugo Chávez, but what populism refers to nowadays in Europe is something else.

L: So what is today's populism?

Q: Today the term is used as a stigma, to indicate the general, and I mean very general, characteristics of political phenomena considered "pathological."

L: So it is a symptom, a sign of crisis...

Q: It doesn't characterize a defined political force, it takes advantage of the alliances it enables, which range from the extreme Right to the radical Left.

L: Therefore it can't solely be considered "rightist"...

Q: I don't think so. It's just as valid for the symbolic unification of Laclau's group, for Pasolini's poor fireflies, for the historical experience of Russian Narodniki in the mid-nineteenth century who intended the redemption of farmers, for Argentinian Peronism, for the jingling handcuffs of Tangentopoli, for the distribution of quarters of a cow, or for National Front's Marine le Pen.

L: What about the Italian neo-populism that followed the crisis of the so-called First Republic?

Q: It's interesting because today Italy is perhaps the only context where populist forces persist in competition with each other, and political communication is dominated by this populist tonality.

L: This includes both the sudden rise of Po Valley localism (Lega Nord) that delivers a decisive blow to the system of mass parties in the years of Tangentopoli, as well as Berlusconi's noisy descent in the telepopulist field, with his ability to mainstream and unify right-wing forces.

Q: There's also the web-populist explosion of M5s that, since the very beginning, has shown an interclassist and non-ideological configuration, able to gather sympathizers of both the radical Left and Right.

L: Many of Berlusconi's populisms have been recovered by Renzi's governmental experience, and Lega has evolved from a nativist tribe to an almost national party like Le Pen.

Q: The split of twenty five years ago has altered Italian populist political grammar and it has never recovered. Even Renzi's Democratic Party is an "institutional populist response to rampant populism."

L: Coming back to the general picture, it doesn't denote an ideology, nor a coherent political style...

Q: ...Nor even a form of governance. It is an attitude of rejection, of existing governmental practices, of the status quo...

L: And of that "centrist-extremism" that has been representing the prevailing constitutional formula. Populism seems to be nothing but an answer, confused but legitimate, to the feeling of abandonment by the classes faced with globalization and rising inequality.

Q: The European Left parties have become instrumental to financial violence, they have bowed to the Fiscal Compact, to austerity policies.

L: How is all of this happening?

Q: Well, its manifestations in Europe are today mostly radically right-wing.

L: . . .ein Gespenst geht um in Europa, ein rechtsextremes.

Q: Referencing "the people" shows that behind populism there is an actively embodied sovereign demand. "Take back control of our borders" has been one of the recurring slogans of Brexit, which is a demand to strengthen the nation-state.

L: Especially nowadays that, after the collapse of all the metanarratives, the epoch is in short supply of -isms, and the most relevant trace of "the people" is the name of the piazza in Rome.

Q: Populism simply serves to outline a certain image, because the People does not exist. There are instead always representations, even antagonistic ones, that privilege some modalities of association, some distinctive traits, some capacities or incapacities: the ethnic people, the herd people, the democratic people, the ignorant people. . .

L: Well, for people, sovereignty, and the state, the recovery of "national sovereignty" is an illusion. What will certainly not be interrupted is the continuity of neoliberalism.

Q: The neoliberal model continues imposing itself automatically, even if consensus has dissolved.

L: What populism masks and at the same time reveals is the great desire of the oligarchy: to govern without people, that is to govern without politics...

Q: The people, the nation, are romantic notions that identify a jumble of subjectivities lacking social solidarity or sympathetic power. The problem that populism can't face, much less solve, is precisely that of solidarity, or rather the recomposition of subjective forces. So the people and nation return as the reactionary attempt of reterritorializing those social forces that have lost any relationship with territoriality.

L: I think I understand what you mean, but it's not enough to say that. Populism is not only romantic, or an attempt to resolidify that which has become deterritorialized, because historically the times when populism worked most was when there was a working class very aware of itself, with many parties competing with each other. Each populism was more than a relation with a nation, it was also a relation with a vision of what kind of abundance will prevail in the future, whether racial, imperial, millenarian, accumulative, austerity. This means it was a kind of ethics.

Q: But what about the populist people or nations?

L: The dominant discourse seems to attribute three essential characteristics: 1) a style of interlocution that directly addresses the people beyond its representatives and its notables; 2) the affirmation that governments and ruling classes are concerned with their own interests more than with public affairs; 3) an identitarian rhetoric that expresses fear and rejection of strangers.

Q: The raw power of numeric superiority, and the ignorance attributed to this numeric superiority.

L: And the racism essential for this construction, but otherwise there isn't any necessary relationship that binds together these three characteristics.

Q: So populism realizes with minimum effort this synthesis between a people hostile to the rulers, and a people becoming enemy to the "others" in general.

L: Right, and when it presents itself in affirmative forms, when it assumes, in other words, a truly existing and already constituted people as its subject, it always ends up claiming boundaries.

Q: The inability to respond in an innovative way to the "crisis of borders" has lead to an ulterior separation of citizens from European institutions, clearly calling into question their legitimacy.

L: Assuming "populism" as a symptom and struggling unrelentingly against its dominant manifestations in Europe basically means referring to a "missing people," and working for the invention of new forms of subjectivity and political action.

Q: There are not many who are explicitly calling themselves "populist."

L: You face yourself in populism.

Q: Maybe it would be easier to try to feel it.

L: Well, first you feel it, before knowing what it is.

Q: Does it come from me, or you, or us?

L: The sophistry seen by Plato is that the science of life, and therefore of government, is able to leverage the "human" inside to organize the "political" outside. It arises from here, to understand what people want, translating the entrails into a universal discourse of the outside, which comes from a part of the self. This is why "populism" is felt with a mixture of familiarity, recognition, and identification, because it comes from you.

Q: Today there is no work, or any aspect of life, that does not require a bit of sophistry from all of us.

L: That's the art of grasping, starting from the affects and the soft parts. Populism is the art of bringing out the others' self, not without an interest of one's own: a wage, a little power, a social position, to hook it to something outside.

Q: Populism is the art of government that best corresponds to the "general intellect at work," since the technical knowledge of our capitalism of intellect is, above all, social knowledge.

L: Yes, but it is also the redemption from shame.

Q: Well, the Western white subjectivity is angrily depressed and, as we said earlier, not very sympathetic.

L: But what do you mean by this? Depression and its subjectivity are no longer simply questions of race. Tinder and metrics are now for everyone.

Q: Yes, but their verbal time is the conditional past, with those phrases like I-could-have, I-should-have, I-would-have-been, which colonize the past from the present. They project the sense of bad economical, biographical, temporal, and affective investments on every possible turning point.

L: Those possibilities that have not been realized are returning at night to assign guilt for the wrong choices that poison your present, and paralyze you from facing the future.

Q: After the dissolution of the Socialist system, the mythology that has taken over is one of absolute and boundless competition, unleashed by neoliberalism in the name of the mythology of enrichment.

L: But this mythology has failed, and the promise of accumulation has worked only for a small part of society. For all the others, the liberal adventure has resulted in precariousness, neuro-exploitation, lower wages, and more labor.

Q: Today automation and so-called artificial intelligence makes living labor marginal, with all those sad passions that accompany it. We live in a time in which the parable described by the substitution of human labor by the intelligent machine reaches its peak.

L: So what's going to happen?

Q: Just what happened with the peasants, the wage earners will become a modest and rather insignificant fraction of the active population. And, paradoxically, masters and trade unionists will have trouble inventing works to guarantee their consent or maintain public order.

L: The refusal of waged labor reappears as a device of capitalist governance now.

Q: If this is the horizon, critical thinking has to abandon any search for a class with which to entrust the fate of revolution. And let go of any residual temptation to make use of the institutions of representation, to take power to do good by force, to accomplish the revolution through the apparatus of the state.

L: We have to try to subtract the affects from the sophists and find a real and true verbal time that allows us to get rid of the obstacle, which is not the heart but the entrails.

Q: I still don't understand what you mean by a real, verbal time though? For me, the more I escape from the grammar of true and false the better I feel. This is not because "the world is relative and plural," but because this is related to a scientific grammar that should be avoided as politics.

L: I'm simply referring to the struggle against the idea of living in the past conditional.

Q: So how to make use of this immense time already freed from wage labor to develop an "attractive work," or rather a gratifying self-fulfilling activity, which encompasses its purpose, where means and ends convert into one another. In short, to let the elective communities emerge.

L: But I don't agree that the elective community is the best thing to defend now. In the last ten years, I have seen no group of affinities work for longer than a year. These communities work within a period of struggle, in the ZAD, in Standing Rock, in the time of an occupation, when you're no longer in a state of aimless negativity. But within our metropolitan time, when our main occupation is to find money, a politics of affinity is really not enough, and can even sometimes be opposed to what we are doing. What you're saying is situated socially within a position where you have free time, but we can't generalize this. I don't think communism is a positive thing that can emerge between us, for me it operates only by the subtraction and reversal that can emerge outside of affective community.

Q: Well elective communities can also refer to something still to come, to use Sandro's words, something referring to the "missing people," the communities everyone is trying to build and feed with their energies because it's what they choose. Your experience of collectivity can be an example of elective community. It's like with Goethe's elective affinities, those you share your life and thoughts and struggles and affection and friendship with. These people, this is a separate thing, its own subtraction and reversal...

— This text is a composition of quotes by Manuel Anselmi, Franco "Bifo" Berardi, Ilaria Bussoni, Augusto Illuminati, Sandro Mezzadra, Thomas Piketty, Cristina Morini, Franco Piperno, Jacques Rancière, and Liaisons.

INDEX

D

E

F

G

H

I

J

K

L

M

N

T

U

V

W

X

Y

Z

We would like to thank Johan Badour, Marion Breton, Hubert Gendron-Blais, Ryan Richardson, Annabelle Rivard, Adrien Tournier, and Laura Thompson for their generous help.

ABOUT LIAISONS

TRANSOCEANIC PARTISAN RESEARCH

More than a collective, less than a world, Liaisons is an inclination, a tangent, a crossroads of confrontations, encounters, and links, with authors from the United States, France, Italy, Japan, Korea, Lebanon, Mexico, Quebec, Russia, and Spain. Liaisons does not study the movement of others as an external object (movement history), nor does it project principles of revolution in the context of pure theory (intellectual history). Instead, it assembles analyses and theorizations directly from the ongoing struggles of affiliated groups, based in different parts of the planet and seeking a common ground. Liaisons has gathered on the basis of long-term friendships and, in ensemble, its discourses shed light on a horizon of living in struggle. The works of Liaisons are not embodiments of a shared doctrine, but rather research on the interconnectivity among singular problems and aspirations, in order to facilitate a planetary reverberation of militant autonomy. The works are to expand along with the permeation of the collective, and metamorphose amidst the fluctuating situation of the world.

liaisons@riseup.net
www.liaisonshq.com

ABOUT COMMON NOTIONS

Common Notions is a publishing house and programming platform that advances new formulations of liberation and living autonomy.

Our books provide timely reflections, clear critiques, and inspiring strategies that amplify movements for social justice.

By any media necessary, we seek to nourish the imagination and generalize common notions about the creation of other worlds beyond state and capital. Our publications trace a constellation of critical and visionary meditations on the organization of freedom. Inspired by various traditions of autonomism and liberation—in the United States and internationally, historically and emerging from contemporary movements—our publications provide resources for a collective reading of struggles past, present, and to come.

Common Notions regularly collaborates with editorial houses, political collectives, militant authors, and visionary designers around the world. Our political and aesthetic interventions are dreamt and realized in collaboration with Antumbra Designs.

www.commonnotions.org
info@commonnotions.org